I0198524

CHARLES DICKENS
AS A LEGAL HISTORIAN

By

William S. Holdsworth
K.C., D.C.L., Hon. LL.D.
Vinerian Professor of Law at Oxford University
Bencher of Lincoln's Inn

THE LAWBOOK EXCHANGE, LTD.
Clark, New Jersey

ISBN-13: 978-1886363069 (cloth)
ISBN-13: 9781616190248 (paperback)

Lawbook Exchange edition 1995, 2010

Printed in the United States of America on acid-free paper

THE LAWBOOK EXCHANGE, LTD.
33 Terminal Avenue
Clark, New Jersey 07066-1321

Please see our website for a selection of our other publications and fine facsimile reprints of classic works of legal history:
www.lawbookexchange.com

Library of Congress Cataloging-in-Publication Data

Holdsworth, William Searle, Sir, 1871-1944.
Charles Dickens as a legal historian / by William S. Holdsworth.
p.cm.
Originally published: New Haven: Yale University Press, 1929.
Includes bibliographical references and index.
ISBN 1-886363-06-4 (cloth: alk. paper)
1. Dickens, Charles, 1812-1870—Knowledge—Law. 2. Dickens, Charles, 1812-1870—Characters—Lawyers.
3. Courts—Great Britain—Historiography. 4. Lawyers in literature. 5. Law in literature.
6. Dickens, Charles, 1812-1870. Bleak House. 7. Dickens, Charles, 1812-1870. Pickwick
papers. I. Title.

PR4592.L3H6 1996
823'.8—dc21 96-465579
CIP

CHARLES DICKENS AS A LEGAL HISTORIAN

By

William S. Holdsworth

K.C., D.C.L., Hon. LL.D.

Vinerian Professor of Law at Oxford University

Bencher of Lincoln's Inn

NEW HAVEN

Yale University Press

1929

Printed in the United States of America

First published, September, 1928
Second printing, January, 1929

Acknowledgment

I wish to thank my wife and Professor Smalley-Baker, Barber Professor of Law in the University of Birmingham, for seeing these Lectures through the press during my absence in India.

W. S. H.

Oxford
April 1928

Contents

Dickens as a Legal Historian

I.

The Courts and the Dwellings of the Lawyers.

MANY of Charles Dickens's novels touch upon the law and lawyers, in some of them the law and lawyers play a considerable part, and in one of them, *Bleak House,* the legal atmosphere is all pervading. Dickens was born in 1812; and the dates of these novels range from 1835 to 1870; so that the law and the lawyers, which Dickens had observed and described, were the law and the lawyers of the first two-thirds of the nineteenth century. That is now a period which has passed into history, and is beginning to attract the attention of historians, legal and otherwise. In these lectures I intend to show you that the treatment by Dickens of various aspects of the law and the lawyers of his day, is a very valuable addition to our authorities, not only for that period, but also for earlier periods in our legal history.

The time at which the scene of many of Dickens's novels is laid dates, in many cases, before the era of reform had begun; and, when he began to write, it had only just begun. Pickwick set out on his travels in 1827, and the book was written in 1836. At the time when Dickens wrote his later works the Legislature had begun, tentatively and cautiously, to make those reforms in the machinery of the law, and in the law itself, which were long overdue. But much still remained to be done. *Bleak House* was written in 1852-1853; and, though some of the abuses there described had been remedied, there was still much which needed reform. Hence in Dickens's descriptions of the courts, the lawyers, and the law of his day, we get an account of those many archaic survivals, which help us to understand earlier periods in the history of our law; we get an account of the way in which the curious mixture of ancient and modern rules, which made up the law of that time, were then worked and applied; and we get an account of the results which they produced. It is obvious that a series of pictures of this age of transition, painted by an exceptionally gifted observer, is of unique value to the legal historian.

There are two main reasons why Dickens's pictures of the courts, the lawyers, and the law of his day have this unique value. In the first place, they give us information which we can get nowhere else. In the second place, these pictures were painted by a man with extraordinary powers of observation, who had first-hand information.

It is always difficult for the legal historian, or, indeed, for any historian, to reconstruct the atmosphere of the period with which he is dealing. From a study of statutes, decided cases, and textbooks we can get a record of what things were actually done. Courts with a certain jurisdiction were established and began to function, the lawyers were educated and organized, and conducted their practices in a particular way, legal rules were originated and developed in certain directions. But it is difficult to get from these authorities an account of how the men of any given period did these things, a picture of the men themselves, or an impression of the contemporary background and the actual scene; and without such an account or such a picture or such an impression our history of events and movements and technical doctrines is a very lifeless story. It is true that in our earlier reports—in the earlier Year Books and even in some of the sixteenth and seventeenth century reports—we get occasionally human touches, and side lights upon the actors—judges, barristers, or litigants; and this is true, very occasionally, of the early statutes. But in later times, when the form of reports and statutes has become stereotyped and impersonal, they cease to give us information of this kind. For these human touches and side lights, which will enable us to see the lawyers at work, and will give us a background and an atmosphere, we must look to other sources —legal and non-legal.

Of the legal writers who have occasionally left us descriptions of their legal world as they saw it, the three most famous are, I think, Fortescue in the fifteenth century, Roger North in the latter part of the seventeenth century, and, in a lesser degree, Romilly in the latter part of the eighteenth century. Fortescue in his *De Laudibus* gives us a description of the legal profession of his day which we get from no other writer. He describes from his own knowledge the mode of the appointment and the daily life of the judges and the serjeants, the Inns of Court and Chancery, their inhabitants, and the mode of legal education. Without his book it would be difficult to piece together, from the Year Books and the records of the Inns, a lifelike picture of the legal profession of his day. Similarly, he gives us an account of the salient features of the common law of his day, which helps to explain why Englishmen, then and later, considered their common law to be one of their most prized possessions. Roger North, the brother of a Lord Keeper and a Chief Justice, knew the legal world of his day from top to bottom. He had a genius for portraiture, and an eye for picturesque scenes. In his Lives of his two brothers, in his Autobiography, and in his *Discourse on the Study of the Laws,* he re-creates the legal scene in which he lived, and peoples it with the lawyers with whom he had been brought into contact. Samuel Romilly, in his memoirs, gives us an account of the life of the law student of his day, of the career of a leading practitioner in the Court of Chancery, and of the efforts of a liberal politician to effect some much needed reforms in the law, at a time when the French Revolution and the Napoleonic Wars had stopped all chance of reform.

Unfortunately we have but few legal writers who have given us the information which Fortescue and North and Romilly have given us. For that information the legal historian is generally obliged to go to non-legal writers—to diarists such as Pepys, to novelists such as Fielding, and to many other sources. He is obliged to read many books, and be thankful if he can dig up, from very miscellaneous sources, a few facts which will help him to put some life into his picture.

But, for the first half of the nineteenth century, the legal historian has in Charles Dickens's novels a source of information which, in its range and lifelike character, is superior to that possessed by the historian of any other period. They supply us with pictures of many phases of the legal world, and re-create its atmosphere.

Dickens was not, it is true, a lawyer. He is not much concerned with the technical rules of law; and he has made at least one bad mistake in his law.* The technical rules which he mentions are rules which strike the imagination by reason of their curiosity. Thus, as Judge Gest has pointed out in his essay on *The Law and Lawyers of Charles Dickens,* he makes fun of the law of dis-

* In *The Old Curiosity Shop* Daniel Quilp commits suicide, and yet Mrs. Quilp, as he had left no will, succeeds to his property. But at that date the property of a felon, including a *felo de se,* was forfeited to the crown; and even if he had not committed suicide his wife could only have succeeded to half his property. As Judge Gest points out (*The Lawyer in Literature,* p. 60), it is not at all clear what right Mrs. Weller had to make a will, as, unless she had a settlement, her property would have passed to her husband on marriage.

tress in *David Copperfield* and in *Bleak House;* of the presumption that if a wife commits a crime in the presence of her husband she is presumed to have done it under his coercion—a doctrine which provoked Bumble to say that "if the law supposes that, the law is an ass"; of the anomalies of the divorce law in *Hard Times;* of suits for brawling in the ecclesiastical courts in *Sketches by Boz.** What Dickens is concerned with is the machinery by which the law was enforced, the men who enforced it, the conditions in which these men lived, and the actual effects of the rules of law, substantive and adjective, upon the men and women of his day. Hence we get in his books that account of the human side of the rules of law and their working, which is essential to the legal historian.

The value of this account is enhanced by the fact that Dickens had both extraordinary powers of observation and first-hand information.

The faculty which especially strikes us in all Dickens's novels is, as Bagehot has said, his power of minute and accurate observation. "We have heard it said that he can go down a crowded street, and tell you all that is in it, what each shop was, what the grocer's name was, how many

* J. M. Gest, *The Lawyer in Literature,* pp. 15-16, 17, 22.

scraps of orange peel there were on the pavement."* It is not strange that no other writer has drawn such wonderful pictures of London. "No other writer has equally comprehended the artistic material which is given by its extent, its aggregation of different elements, its mouldiness, its brilliancy."† "He describes his London like a special correspondent for posterity."‡ And this talent for observation was applied as much to personal characteristics as to external surroundings. "The boots at the inn, the pick-pockets in the street, the undertaker, the Mrs. Gamp, are all of them at his disposal."§ He takes, as Bagehot says, a special trait and makes a complete character out of it. Hence we do not find in Dickens's novels many absolutely natural characters. They are often caricatures. But we do find the characteristics of certain persons of certain callings, described in a manner which enables us to see certain types of the men who were pursuing those callings in Dickens's own day. Both the men themselves, and the environment in which they worked, are described with a minuteness which stamps on the memory an indelible impression.

* *Literary Studies,* II, 194.
† *Ibid.,* II, 195.
‡ *Ibid.,* II, 197.
§ *Ibid.,* II, 197.

Now, what is important for us is the fact that Dickens's early history and training led him to employ these powers on the lawyers and their environment. At the age of twelve he visited his father who had been imprisoned for debt in the Marshalsea prison; and, as his works show, this left an indelible impression on his mind. At the age of fifteen he was in the office of Charles Molloy, an attorney of 6 Symond's Inn, and afterwards in the office of Ellis and Blackmore, attorneys of 1 Raymond's Buildings, Gray's Inn.* He had been a reporter in the Doctors' Commons and in Lord Chancellor Lyndhurst's Court at the age of eighteen; and in 1844 he had been the victorious plaintiff in five Chancery suits against certain publishers who had pirated the *Christmas Carol*.† Throughout his life he numbered famous lawyers amongst his friends. One of these lawyers, Serjeant Thomas Noon Talfourd, is specially connected with him. Thomas Noon Talfourd was the editor of Charles Lamb's works and letters, the

* But see E. T. Jaques, *Charles Dickens in Chancery*, p. 12, who thinks that the clerkship to Molloy came after that to Ellis and Blackmore.

† See *ibid.*; these proceedings did not extend, as Forster says, to the pirates of *Martin Chuzzlewit*, *ibid.*, p. 59.

author of the first Copyright Act, and one of Dickens's counsel in his Chancery actions against piratical publishers. He revised the trial scene in *Pickwick,* and to him *Pickwick* was dedicated.* Moreover he was the occasion of a joke to which Dickens alludes in *Pickwick.* He was the last of a batch of serjeants, created in 1833, to whom precedence was given next after the existing King's Counsel. The next batch of King's Counsel were given precedence next after Thomas *Noon* Talfourd. Hence they were called the post-meridians or the after-noons.† This was the foundation of Mr. Peter Magnus's remark to Pickwick that his initials being P.M. he often signed himself in notes to his friends as *Afternoon.*‡ It is not surprising, therefore, that Dickens should have employed his wonderful powers of observation on the pageant of the law. His novels are a gallery of pictures of the life of the law in his own day. As Mr. Theobald Mathew has said,§ the modern lawyer

is only dimly aware that there were once such things

* P. Fitzgerald, *Bardell* v. *Pickwick,* p. 85 n.

† Foss, *Judges,* IX, 66.

‡ See *Law Quarterly Review,* XXXIV, 322.

§ *Ibid.,* p. 320.

as the Courts of Westminster, the three "Chiefs," Guildhall Sittings, Postmen and Tubmen, Barons of the Exchequer, and Serjeants-at-law. If desirous of information about these ghosts, he turns to the small group of practitioners who were called to the Bar in the 'seventies, and obtains it in a more or less accurate form. Being of this generation, he probably does not read "Pickwick." Were he to do so, he would realize that in the pages of that immortal work are faithfully recorded fragments of legal history which fallible human memory cannot be expected to retain, and that the story of the suit for breach of promise of marriage brought by Mrs. Bardell, widow, against Samuel Pickwick, gentleman, is a mine of useful information to the antiquarian. Has not the time come for an annotated edition of that masterpiece, to which the student-at-law may be referred by readers and lecturers for a reliable account of the practical working of the law of personal actions when Queen Victoria ascended the throne?

I propose in these lectures to show how, not only *Pickwick,* but also many of the other novels of Charles Dickens, can be used to illustrate the legal history of his period. In this lecture I shall speak of the external conditions in which the law was administered—the courts and the dwellings of the lawyers. In my second lecture I shall speak of the types of lawyers, lawyers' clerks, and other satellites of the law, which Dickens has sketched for us. In my third lecture I shall speak of *Bleak House* and the procedure of the Court of Chancery. In my last lecture I shall speak of *Pickwick* and the procedure of the common law.

In dealing with this subject—the courts and the dwellings of the lawyers—I shall speak first of the central courts of common law, and the courts held by the commissioners of Oyer and Terminer and Gaol Delivery at the Old Bailey; secondly, of the Court of Chancery; thirdly, of the Insolvent Court; fourthly, of the offices of the courts; fifthly, of Doctors' Commons; and lastly of the dwellings of the lawyers.

The central courts of common law at Westminster do not figure very largely in Dickens's novels. At the time when he wrote, the courts surrounding Westminster Hall had been remodelled by Soane.* At the time when the action of *The Pickwick Papers* takes place this remodelling was nearly complete. The new courts were opened in 1828, and "except as regards certain alterations of

* I have taken these particulars from E. T. Jaques, *Charles Dickens in Chancery*, pp. 20-23.

detail in the upper floors, Soane's courts underwent no change till they were pulled down in or about 1884." These buildings accommodated the three courts of common law, the Bail Court, the Court of the Vice-Chancellor of England, and the Lord Chancellor's Court. On an upper floor was the Court of the Master of the Rolls, and the Court of a second Vice-Chancellor—familiarly known as the "dog hole." The third Vice-Chancellor's Court was on the floor above, and was familiarly known as the "Cock-loft." Mr. Roscoe has told us that in 1860 the Court of Admiralty was transferred from Doctors' Commons to this "Cock-loft."*

It may seem strange that Dickens has left us no description of the Court of Common Pleas, seeing that the famous case of *Bardell* v. *Pickwick* was begun in that court. But Mr. Jackson of the firm of Dodson and Fogg, when he subpœnaed Snodgrass, Tupman, Winkle, and Sam Weller, said that the case was to come on "in the sittens after Term, fourteenth of Febooary, we expect."† If the case had come on in term time it would have been heard in the Court of Common Pleas. But,

* *The High Court of Admiralty, The Last Phase,* p. 4.
† That is, Feb. 14, 1828. *Pickwick,* chap. xxxi.

as the legal terms were much too short for the business to be done, the judges were accustomed to sit after the term at Serjeant's Inn. An Act of 1823 had given statutory sanction to this practice, and allowed the judges to sit there or at "some other convenient place." It was by virtue of that Act that the case was heard at the Guildhall.*

No better description has ever been given of a court, just before the business of the day is begun, than Dickens's description of the court in the Guildhall on the day of the hearing of Mrs. Bardell's action: †

> "Lowten," said Perker, when they reached the outer hall of the court, "put Mr. Pickwick's friends in the students' box; Mr. Pickwick himself had better sit by me. This way, my dear sir, this way." Taking Mr. Pickwick by the coat-sleeve, the little man led him to the low seat just beneath the desks of the King's Counsel, which is constructed for the convenience of attorneys, who from that spot can whisper into the ear of the leading counsel in the case any instructions that may be necessary during the progress of the trial. The occupants of this seat are invisible to the great body of spectators, inasmuch as they sit on a much lower

* See *Law Quarterly Review,* XXXIV, 320-321.

† *Pickwick,* chap. xxxiv.

level than either the barristers or the audience, whose seats are raised above the floor. Of course they have their backs to both, and their faces towards the judge.

"That's the witness-box, I suppose?" said Mr. Pickwick, pointing to a kind of pulpit, with a brass rail, on his left hand.

"That's the witness-box, my dear sir," replied Perker, disinterring a quantity of papers from the blue bag, which Lowten had just deposited at his feet.

"And that," said Mr. Pickwick, pointing to a couple of enclosed seats on his right, "that's where the jurymen sit, is it not?"

"The identical place, my dear sir," replied Perker, tapping the lid of his snuff-box.

Mr. Pickwick stood up in a state of great agitation, and took a glance at the court. There were already a pretty large sprinkling of spectators in the gallery, and a numerous muster of gentlemen in wigs, in the barristers' seats, who presented, as a body, all that pleasing and extensive variety of nose and whisker for which the bar of England is so justly celebrated. Such of the gentlemen as had a brief to carry, carried it in as conspicuous a manner as possible, and occasionally scratched their noses therewith, to impress the fact more strongly on the observation of the spectators. Other gentlemen, who had no briefs to show, carried under their arms goodly octavos, with a red label behind, and that underdone-pie-crust-coloured cover, which is technically known as "law calf." Others, who had neither briefs nor books, thrust their hands into their pockets, and looked as wise as they conveniently could; others, again, moved here and there with great restlessness and earnestness of manner, content to awaken thereby the admiration and astonishment of the uninitiated strangers. The whole, to the great wonderment of Mr. Pickwick, were divided into little groups, who were chatting and discussing the news of the day in the most unfeeling manner possible,—just as if no trial at all were coming on.

It may be noted that the box for the accommodation of the students was an old and familiar feature of the courts. From the reign of Edward I onwards, attendance at court had been an essential feature of the education of the law student. We read in the Year Books of Edward II's reign of the "Crib," which seems to have been its mediæval prototype.* Roger North describes to us the manner in which Hale would explain the law for the benefit of the students;† and a famous tale told by Lord Campbell about Lord Kenyon shows that the students' box was inhabited by students in the eighteenth and early nineteenth centuries.‡

* *Y.B.* 3, 4 Ed., II (S.S.), xli-xlii.

† *Discourse on the Study of the Laws,* pp. 32-33.

‡ *Lives of the Chief Justices,* III, 85 n.

But not much law can be extracted from a breach of promise action, and so the students' box was on this occasion available for the accommodation of Mr. Pickwick's friends.

Of the trials held by the commissioners of Oyer and Terminer and Gaol Delivery at the Old Bailey, Dickens has given us a description in the trial of Christopher Nubbles in *The Old Curiosity Shop.** There is nothing, however, very noteworthy in this description. Much more noteworthy is his description of the surroundings of the Old Bailey which he has given us in *Great Expectations,*† and of some of its characteristics at an earlier date in *A Tale of Two Cities.*‡

Here is the description given in *Great Expectations:*

> I saw the great black dome of Saint Paul's bulging at me from behind a grim stone building which a bystander said was Newgate Prison. Following the wall of the jail, I found the roadway covered with straw to deaden the noise of passing vehicles; and from this, and from the quantity of people standing about, smelling strongly of spirits and beer, I inferred that the trials were on.

* Chap. lxiii. † Chap. xx.
‡ Bk. II, chap. ii.

While I looked about me here, an exceedingly dirty and partially drunk minister of justice asked me if I would like to step in and hear a trial or so: informing me that he could give me a front place for half-a-crown, whence I should command a full view of the Lord Chief Justice in his wig and robes—mentioning that awful personage like a waxwork, and presently offering him at the reduced price of eighteenpence. As I declined the proposal on the plea of an appointment, he was so good as to take me into a yard and show me where the gallows was kept, and also where people were publicly whipped, and then he showed me the Debtors' Door, out of which culprits came to be hanged; heightening the interest of that dreadful portal by giving me to understand that "four on 'em" would come out at that door the day after to-morrow at eight in the morning to be killed in a row.

Here is the description given in *A Tale of Two Cities*.

They hanged at Tyburn, in those days, so the street outside Newgate had not obtained one infamous notoriety that has since attached to it. But, the gaol was a vile place, in which most kinds of debauchery and villainy were practised, and where dire diseases were bred, that came into court with the prisoners, and sometimes rushed straight from the dock at my Lord Chief Justice himself, and pulled him off the bench. It had more than once happened, that the Judge in the black cap pronounced his own doom as certainly as the prisoner's, and even died before him. For the rest, the Old Bailey was famous as a kind of deadly inn-yard, from which pale travellers set out continually, in carts and coaches, on a violent passage into the other world.

In term time the Court of Chancery sat at Westminster. Out of term it sat in the old hall of Lincoln's Inn. When Dickens wrote, the old hall was a rather mean looking building covered with stucco; and, till the other day, it looked much the same, except that the colonnade, under which Kenge and Esther Summerson passed to the Lord Chancellor's private room, had disappeared. But its mean appearance is largely due to its coat of stucco. It is in fact the oldest of the existing halls of the Inns of Court; and it is now being restored to its original condition. The stucco is being stripped off, and the Tudor brick and stone work revealed. The plaster ceiling has been removed, and the old open work timber roof uncovered. When the work is finished it will be a handsome and interesting relic of the early Tudor period.

Dickens has left us pictures of the Court of Chancery at Lincoln's Inn, and of the scene in

Westminster Hall, outside the court, on the day that the great case of *Jarndyce* v. *Jarndyce* came to an end. His picture of the court at Lincoln's Inn is in his famous opening chapter of *Bleak House.*

The raw afternoon is rawest, and the dense fog is densest, and the muddy streets are muddiest, near that leaden-headed old obstruction, appropriate ornament for the threshold of a leaden-headed old corporation: Temple Bar. And hard by Temple Bar, in Lincoln's Inn Hall, at the very heart of the fog, sits the Lord High Chancellor in his High Court of Chancery.

On such an afternoon, if ever, the Lord High Chancellor ought to be sitting here—as here he is—with a foggy glory round his head, softly fenced in with crimson cloth and curtains, addressed by a large advocate with great whiskers, a little voice, and an interminable brief, and outwardly directing his contemplation to the lantern in the roof, where he can see nothing but fog. On such an afternoon, some score of members of the High Court of Chancery bar ought to be—as here they are—mistily engaged in one of the ten thousand stages of an endless cause, tripping one another up on slippery precedents, groping knee-deep in technicalities, running their goat-hair and horse-hair warded heads against walls of words, and making a pretence of equity with serious faces, as players might. On such an afternoon, the various solicitors in the cause, some two or three of whom have inherited it from their fathers, who made a fortune by it, ought to be—as are they not?—ranged in a line, in a long matted well (but you might look in vain for Truth at the bottom of it), between the registrar's red table and the silk gowns, with bills, cross-bills, answers, rejoinders, injunctions, affidavits, issues, references to masters, masters' reports, mountains of costly nonsense, piled before them.

His picture of the scene outside the court at Westminster is at the end of *Bleak House*.*

When we came to Westminster Hall, we found that the day's business was begun. Worse than that, we found such an unusual crowd in the Court of Chancery that it was full to the door, and we could neither see nor hear what was passing within. It appeared to be something droll, for occasionally there was a laugh, a cry of "Silence!" It appeared to be something interesting, for every one was pushing and striving to get nearer. It appeared to be something that made the professional gentlemen very merry, for there were several young counsellors in wigs and whiskers on the outside of the crowd, and when one of them told the others about it, they put their hands in their pockets, and quite doubled themselves up with laughter, and went stamping about the pavement of the hall.

* Chap. lxv.

We asked a gentleman by us, if he knew what cause was on? He told us Jarndyce and Jarndyce. We asked him if he knew what was doing in it? He said, really no he did not, nobody ever did; but as well as he could make out, it was over. Over for the day? we asked him. No, he said; over for good.

A break up soon took place in the crowd, and the people came streaming out looking flushed and hot, and bringing a quantity of bad air with them. Still they were all exceedingly amused, and were more like people coming out from a Farce or a Juggler than from a court of Justice. We stood aside, watching for any countenance we knew; and presently great bundles of paper began to be carried out—bundles in bags, bundles too large to be got into any bags, immense masses of papers of all shapes and no shapes, which the bearers staggered under, and threw down for the time being, anyhow, on the Hall pavement, while they went back to bring out more. Even these clerks were laughing. We glanced at the papers, and seeing Jarndyce and Jarndyce everywhere, asked an official-looking person who was standing in the midst of them, whether the cause was over. "Yes," he said; "it was all up with it at last!" and burst out laughing too.

The facility with which it was possible to arrest for non-payment of debt,* and the fact that the

* As to this see below, pp. 136-138.

bankruptcy laws applied only to traders, had made it necessary for the Legislature to pass from time to time acts for the relief of insolvent debtors. A permanent act, passed in 1813,* created a court for the relief of insolvent debtors, which sat in Portugal Street, Lincoln's Inn Fields.† We get in *Pickwick* a picture of its actual appearance, and of the practitioners before it, which only Dickens could have drawn.‡

In a lofty room, ill-lighted and worse ventilated, situate in Portugal Street, Lincoln's Inn Fields, there sit nearly the whole year round, one, two, three, or four gentlemen in wigs, as the case may be, with little writing desks before them, constructed after the fashion of those used by the judges of the land, barring the French polish. There is a box of barristers on their right hand; there is an inclosure of insolvent debtors on their left; and there is an inclined plane of most especially dirty faces in their front. These gentlemen are the Commissioners of the Insolvent Court, and the place in which they sit, is the Insolvent Court itself.

It is, and has been, time out of mind, the remarkable fate of this Court to be, somehow or other, held and understood, by the general consent of all the desti-

* 53 George III, c. 102.

† See 1 & 2 Victoria, c. 110, §28.

‡ Chap. xliii.

tute shabby-genteel people in London, as their common resort, and place of daily refuge. It is always full. The steams of beer and spirits perpetually ascend to the ceiling, and, being condensed by the heat, roll down the walls like rain; there are more old suits of clothes in it at one time, than will be offered for sale in all Houndsditch in a twelvemonth; more unwashed skins and grizzly beards than all the pumps and shaving-shops between Tyburn and Whitechapel could render decent, between sunrise and sunset.

It must not be supposed that any of these people have the least shadow of business in, or the remotest connection with, the place they so indefatigably attend. If they had, it would be no matter of surprise, and the singularity of the thing would cease. Some of them sleep during the greater part of the sitting; others carry small portable dinners wrapped in pocket-handkerchiefs or sticking out of their worn-out pockets, and munch and listen with equal relish; but no one among them was ever known to have the slightest personal interest in any case that was ever brought forward. Whatever they do, there they sit from the first moment to the last. When it is heavy rainy weather, they all come in, wet through; and at such times the vapours of the Court are like those of a fungus-pit.

A casual visitor might suppose this place to be a Temple dedicated to the Genius of Seediness. There is not a messenger or process-server attached to it, who wears a coat that was made for him; not a tolerably fresh, or wholesome-looking man in the whole establishment, except a little white-headed apple-faced tipstaff, and even he, like an ill-conditioned cherry preserved in brandy, seems to have artificially dried and withered up into a state of preservation to which he can lay no natural claim. The very barristers' wigs are ill-powdered, and their curls lack crispness.

When Dickens wrote, and indeed till the opening of the Royal Courts of Justice in 1884, the offices of the courts were scattered all over London.* The offices of the Court of Chancery and of the Court of the Master of the Rolls were to be found in the Inns and lanes adjoining Chancery Lane. The Masters' offices of the King's Bench were in the Temple; those of the Common Pleas were in Serjeant's Inn and Chancery Lane; those of the Exchequer were in Stone Buildings, Lincoln's Inn. It is to these offices that Dickens alludes in the following passage from *Pickwick:*†

Scattered about in various holes and corners of the Temple, are certain dark and dirty chambers, in and out of which, all the morning in Vacation, and half the

* *Parlt. Papers* (1860), vol. XXXI. Report on the expediency of bringing together the courts of law and equity, §7.

† Chap. xxxi.

evening too in term time, there may be seen constantly hurrying with bundles of papers under their arms, and protruding from their pockets, an almost uninterrupted succession of lawyers' clerks. . . . These sequestered nooks are the public offices of the legal profession, where writs are issued, judgments signed, declarations filed, and numerous other ingenious machines put in motion for the torture and torment of His Majesty's liege subjects, and for the comfort and emolument of the practitioners of the law. They are for the most part low roofed, mouldy rooms, where innumerable rolls of parchment, which have been perspiring in secret for the last century, send forth an agreeable odour, which is mingled by day with the scent of the dry rot, and by night with the various exhalations which arise from damp cloaks, festering umbrellas, and the coarsest tallow candles.

Of the offices of the Court of Common Pleas at Serjeant's Inn we have a more particular description. Mr. Pickwick was taken in execution for non-payment of the damages and costs which had been awarded against him. Being taken by the sheriff, he must either remain in the sheriff's custody and go to the prison in Whitecross Street, or be removed by writ of *habeas corpus* to the Fleet prison. Whitecross Street, as Perker pointed out, was impossible—"sixty beds in a ward; and the bolt's on sixteen hours out of the twenty-four."* So it was determined that he should go to the Fleet. To get the *habeas corpus* to remove him to the Fleet it was necessary to go to the Judge's Chambers at Serjeant's Inn. The office of the Judge's clerk

was a room of specially dirty appearance, with a very low ceiling and old panelled walls; and so badly lighted, that although it was broad day outside, great tallow candles were burning on the desks. At one end, was a door leading to the judge's private apartment, round which were congregated a crowd of attorneys and managing clerks, who were called in, in the order in which their respective appointments stood upon the file. Every time this door was opened to let a party out, the next party made a violent rush to get in; and, as in addition to the numerous dialogues which passed between the gentlemen who were waiting to see the judge, a variety of personal squabbles ensued between the greater part of those who had seen him, there was as much noise as could well be raised in an apartment of such confined dimensions.

Nor were the conversations of these gentlemen the only sounds that broke upon the ear. Standing on a box behind a wooden bar at another end of the room,

* Chap. xl.

was a clerk in spectacles, who was "taking the affidavits": large batches of which were, from time to time, carried into the private room by another clerk for the judge's signature. There were a large number of attorneys' clerks to be sworn, and it being a moral impossibility to swear them all at once, the struggles of these gentlemen to reach the clerk in spectacles, were like those of a crowd to get in at the pit door of a theatre when Gracious Majesty honours it with its presence.

For example. Leaning against the wall, close beside the seat Mr. Pickwick had taken, was an office-lad of fourteen, with a tenor voice; near him, a common-law clerk with a bass one.

A clerk hurried in with a bundle of papers, and stared about him.

"Sniggle and Blink," cried the tenor.

"Porkin and Snob," growled the bass.

"Stumpy and Deacon," said the new comer.

Nobody answered; the next man who came in, was hailed by the whole three; and he in his turn shouted for another firm; and then somebody else roared in a loud voice for another; and so forth.

All this time, the man in spectacles was hard at work, swearing the clerks: the oath being invariably administered, without any effort at punctuation, and usually in the following terms:

"Take the book in your right hand this is your

name and hand-writing you swear that the contents of this your affidavit are true so help you God a shilling you must get change I haven't got it."

Now compare this description with that of a witness who gave evidence before the Common Law Procedure Commissioners in 1831. Mr. Thomas Lott, an attorney, said, "the rule office on the first day of term is a perfect bear garden; and when there has been a great pressure of business, and those dirty little holes, the judges' chambers, much crowded, I have seen oaths administered through the window to deponents in the court-yard, and persons excepting to bail compelled to make their exit through a back window rather than encounter the crowd."*

Judges' Chambers, as Mr. Theobald Mathew has pointed out, survived in much the same condition till the opening of the Royal Courts of Justice. "Parliament, not long after *Bardell* v. *Pickwick* had been disposed of, was petitioned in vain to provide more seemly quarters, and the squalor, the crowd, and the fight to get into the judge's room were features of a barrister's daily work till 1882."†

* *Parlt. Papers* (1831), vol. X, App. C., p. 146.
† *Law Quarterly Review,* XXXIV, 327-328.

Doctors' Commons, situated close by St. Paul's Cathedral, was the dwelling of the proctors and advocates,* whose practice lay in the Ecclesiastical, the Admiralty, and the Prize Courts. Here is a description of Doctors' Commons, and of these proctors and advocates and their practice:†

"What *is* a proctor, Steerforth?" said I.

"Why, he is a sort of monkish attorney," replied Steerforth. "He is, to some faded courts held in Doctors' Commons—a lazy old nook near St. Paul's Churchyard—what solicitors are to the courts of law and equity. He is a functionary whose existence, in the natural course of things, would have terminated about two hundred years ago. I can tell you best what he is, by telling you what Doctors' Commons is. It's a little out-of-the-way place, where they administer what is called ecclesiastical law, and play all kinds of tricks with obsolete old monsters of acts of Parliament, which three-fourths of the world know nothing about, and the other fourth supposes to have been dug up, in a fossil state, in the days of the Edwards. It's a place that has an ancient monopoly in suits about people's wills and people's marriages, and disputes among ships and boats."

* The advocates were the equivalent of the barristers, and the proctors of the attorneys and solicitors.

† *David Copperfield,* chap. xxiii.

"Nonsense, Steerforth!" I exclaimed. "You don't mean to say that there is any affinity between nautical matters and ecclesiastical matters?"

"I don't, indeed, my dear boy," he returned; "but I mean to say that they are managed and decided by the same set of people, down in that same Doctors' Commons. You shall go there one day, and find them blundering through half the nautical terms in Young's Dictionary, apropos of the 'Nancy' having run down the 'Sarah Jane,' or Mr. Peggotty and the Yarmouth boatmen having put off in a gale of wind with an anchor and cable to the 'Nelson' Indiaman in distress; and you shall go there another day, and find them deep in the evidence, pro and con., respecting a clergyman who has misbehaved himself; and you shall find the judge in the nautical case, the advocate in the clergyman's case, or contrariwise. They are like actors: now a man's a judge, and now he is not a judge; now he's one thing, now he's another! now he's something else, change and change about; but it's always a very pleasant, profitable little affair of private theatricals, presented to an uncommonly select audience."

"But advocates and proctors are not one and the same?" said I, a little puzzled. "Are they?"

"No," returned Steerforth, "the advocates are civilians—men who have taken a doctor's degree at college—which is the first reason of my knowing anything about it. The proctors employ the advocates. Both get very comfortable fees, and altogether they make a mighty snug little party. On the whole, I would recommend you to take to Doctors' Commons kindly, David. They plume themselves on their gentility there, I can tell you, if that's any satisfaction."

The buildings described by Dickens had been created after the Fire of London, and consisted of two quadrangles and a garden. In these two quadrangles were the chambers of the advocates and proctors, a hall, and a library. The courts—Ecclesiastical, Prize, or Admiralty—sat in the hall. Dickens's description of a court held in the hall is a masterpiece.*

Mr. Spenlow conducted me through a paved courtyard formed of grave brick houses, which I inferred, from the Doctors' names upon the doors, to be the official abiding-places of the learned advocates of whom Steerforth had told me; and into a large dull room, not unlike a chapel to my thinking, on the left hand. The upper part of this room was fenced off from the rest; and there, on the two sides of a raised platform of the horse-shoe form, sitting on easy old-fashioned dining-room chairs, were sundry gentlemen in red gowns and grey wigs, whom I found to be the

* *David Copperfield,* chap. xxiii.

Doctors aforesaid. Blinking over a little desk like a pulpit-desk, in the curve of the horse-shoe, was an old gentleman, whom, if I had seen him in an aviary, I should certainly have taken for an owl, but who, I learned, was the presiding judge. In the space within the horse-shoe, lower than these, that is to say on about the level of the floor, were sundry other gentlemen of Mr. Spenlow's rank, and dressed like him in black gowns with white fur upon them, sitting at a long green table. Their cravats were in general stiff, I thought, and their looks haughty; but in this last respect, I presently conceived I had done them an injustice, for when two or three of them had to rise and answer a question of the presiding dignitary, I never saw anything more sheepish. The public, represented by a boy with a comforter, and a shabby-genteel man secretly eating crumbs out of his coat pockets, was warming itself at a stove in the centre of the Court. The languid stillness of the place was only broken by the chirping of this fire and by the voice of one of the Doctors, who was wandering slowly through a perfect library of evidence, and stopping to put up, from time to time, at little road-side inns of argument on the journey. Altogether, I have never, on any occasion, made one at such a cosey, dosey, old-fashioned, time-forgotten, sleepy-headed little family-party in all my life; and I felt it would be quite a soothing opiate to belong to it in any character—except perhaps as a suitor.

Equally good is his account of the Prerogative Office, where wills were insecurely kept, and the work was done by poorly paid clerks, while sinecurists received magnificent revenues.*

I submitted that I thought the Prerogative Office rather a queerly managed institution. Mr. Spenlow inquired in what respect? I replied, with all due deference to his experience (but with more deference, I am afraid, to his being Dora's father), that perhaps it was a little nonsensical that the Registry of that Court, containing the original wills of all persons leaving effects within the immense province of Canterbury, for three whole centuries, should be an accidental building, never designed for the purpose, leased by the registrars for their own private emolument, unsafe, not even ascertained to be fireproof, choked with the important documents it held, and positively, from the roof to the basement, a mercenary speculation of the registrars, who took great fees from the public, and crammed the public's wills away anyhow and anywhere, having no other object than to get rid of them cheaply. That, perhaps, it was a little unreasonable that these registrars in the receipt of profits amounting to eight or nine thousand pounds a year (to say nothing of the profits of the deputy registrars, and clerks of seats), should not be obliged to spend a little of that money,

* *David Copperfield,* chap. xxxiii.

in finding a reasonably safe place for the important documents which all classes of people were compelled to hand over to them, whether they would or no. That, perhaps, it was a little unjust, that all the great offices in this great office should be magnificent sinecures, while the unfortunate working-clerks, in the cold dark room up-stairs were the worst rewarded, and the least considered men, doing important services, in London. That perhaps it was a little indecent that the principal registrar of all, whose duty it was to find the public, constantly resorting to this place, all needful accommodation, should be an enormous sinecurist in virtue of that post (and might be, besides, a clergyman, a pluralist, the holder of a stall in a cathedral, and what not), while the public was put to the inconvenience of which we had a specimen every afternoon when the office was busy, and which we knew to be quite monstrous. That, perhaps, in short, this Prerogative Office of the diocese of Canterbury was altogether such a pestilent job, and such a pernicious absurdity, that but for its being squeezed away in a corner of Saint Paul's Churchyard, which few people knew, it must have been turned completely inside out, and upside down, long ago.

Then, too, there is the account of the scene at the entrance of the Commons, where "kidnappers and inveiglers were planted . . . with instructions to do their utmost to cut off all persons in mourning (probate business), and all gentlemen with anything bashful in their appearance (matrimonial business), and entice them to the offices of their respective employers."* Mr. Tony Weller was the victim of one of these inveiglers, and, having been induced to buy a marriage license, he felt himself obliged, in order not to waste it, to propose to Mrs. Clarke, the widow.†

Dickens has left us several pictures of the Inns of Court, and of those satellites of the Inns of Court—the Inns of Chancery, which have now for the most part disappeared. He has also left us several pictures of the interior of the lawyers' offices.

What a picture of the human side of the Inns of Court is contained in the following passage from *Pickwick:*‡

"Aha!" said the old man, "Aha! who was talking about the Inns?"

"I was, sir," replied Mr. Pickwick; "I was observing what singular old places they are."

"*You!*" said the old man, contemptuously, "What

* *David Copperfield,* chap. xxxix.

† *Pickwick,* chap. x.

‡ Chap. xxi.

do *you* know of the time when young men shut themselves up in those lonely rooms, and read and read, hour after hour, and night after night, till their reason wandered beneath their midnight studies; till their mental powers were exhausted; till morning's light brought no freshness or health to them; and they sank beneath the unnatural devotion of their youthful energies to their dry old books? Coming down to a later time, and a very different day, what do *you* know of the gradual sinking beneath consumption, or the quick wasting of fever—the grand results of 'life' and dissipation—which men have undergone in these same rooms? How many vain pleaders for mercy, do you think, have turned away heart-sick from the lawyer's office, to find a resting-place in the Thames, or a refuge in the gaol? They are no ordinary houses, those. There is not a panel in the old wainscotting, but what, if it were endowed with the powers of speech and memory, could start from the wall, and tell its tale of horror—the romance of life, sir, the romance of life! Common-place as they may seem now, I tell you they are strange old places, and I would rather hear many a legend with a terrific sounding name, than the true history of one old set of chambers."

Symond's Inn, one of the Inns of Chancery, where Dickens had served as clerk to Charles Molloy, he describes as "a little, pale, wall-eyed, woe-begone inn, like a large dust-bin of two compartments and a sifter. It looks as if Symond were a sparing man in his way, and constructed his inn of old building materials, which took kindly to the dry rot and to dirt, and all things decaying and dismal, and perpetuated Symond's name with congenial shabbiness."* Barnard's Inn is described in *Great Expectations:*†

I had supposed that establishment to be an hotel kept by Mr. Barnard, to which the Blue Boar in our town was a mere public-house. Whereas I now found Barnard to be a disembodied spirit, or a fiction, and his inn the dingiest collection of shabby buildings ever squeezed together in a rank corner as a club for tomcats.

We entered this haven through a wicket-gate, and were disgorged by an introductory passage into a melancholy little square that looked to me like a flat burying-ground. I thought it had the most dismal trees in it, and the most dismal sparrows, and the most dismal cats, and the most dismal houses (in number half a dozen or so), that I had ever seen. I thought the windows of the sets of chambers into which those houses were divided, were in every stage of dilapidated blind and curtain, crippled flower-pot, cracked glass,

* *Bleak House,* chap. xxxix. † Chap. xxi.

dusty decay, and miserable makeshift; while To Let To Let To Let, glared at me from empty rooms, as if no new wretches ever came there, and the vengeance of the soul of Barnard were being slowly appeased by the gradual suicide of the present occupants and their unholy interment under the gravel. A frouzy morning of soot and smoke attired this forlorn creation of Barnard, and it had strewed ashes on its head, and was undergoing penance and humiliation as a mere dust-hole.

Dickens has left us many pictures of the interiors of lawyers' offices. There are Serjeant Snubbin's Chambers, to which Mr. Pickwick insists on penetrating—littered with books of practice and papers, its furniture old and rickety and dusty, showing that the Serjeant "was far too much occupied with his professional pursuits to take any great heed or regard of his personal comforts."* There is the great Mr. Tulkinghorn's office and residence combined in Lincoln's Inn Fields.† There are Kenge and Carboy's offices in Lincoln's Inn—dusty and dark‡—and Spenlow and Jorkins's offices in Doctors' Commons.§ There

* *Pickwick,* chap. xxxi.

† *Bleak House,* chap. x.

‡ *Ibid.,* chap. iii.

§ *David Copperfield,* chap. xxiii.

are the shabby offices of that great criminal lawyer, Mr. Jaggers, which were adorned with the busts of two of his clients who had ended their lives on the gallows, and with other articles reminiscent of past criminal cases in which he had been engaged.* There are the offices of a firm of country solicitors—Snitchey and Craggs: †

> The offices of Messrs. Snitchey and Craggs stood convenient, with an open door down two smooth steps, in the market-place; so that any angry farmer inclining towards hot water, might tumble into it at once. Their special council-chamber and hall of conference was an old back-room up-stairs, with a low dark ceiling, which seemed to be knitting its brows gloomily in the consideration of tangled points of law. It was furnished with some high-backed leathern chairs, garnished with great goggle-eyed brass nails, of which, every here and there, two or three had fallen out—or had been picked out, perhaps, by the wandering thumbs and forefingers of bewildered clients. There was a framed print of a great judge in it, every curl in whose dreadful wig had made a man's hair stand on end. Bales of papers filled the dusty closet, shelves, and tables; and round the wainscot there were tiers of boxes, padlocked and fireproof, with people's names

* *Great Expectations,* chaps. xx and xxiv.

† *The Battle of Life,* part ii.

painted outside, which anxious visitors felt themselves, by a cruel enchantment, obliged to spell backwards and forwards, and to make anagrams of, while they sat, seeming to listen to Snitchey and Craggs, without comprehending one word of what they said.

These illustrations show that we have in Dickens's novels a wonderful picture of the environment in which the lawyers of the early Victorian period did their work. We shall see, in the following lecture, that Dickens has given us a no less wonderful picture of the lawyers, their clerks, and other satellites of the law.

II.

The Lawyers, Lawyers' Clerks, and Other Satellites of the Law.

DICKENS's practical acquaintance with the law in the offices of Charles Molloy, and Ellis and Blackmore, had given him an extensive knowledge of the lower ranks of the legal profession. He knew well the sheriffs' officers, the law stationers, and the hack copyists whom the law stationers employed. He had an equally wide acquaintance with many different types of attorneys and solicitors. But his knowledge of the higher ranks of the legal profession is less extensive. Neither barristers nor king's counsel play any great part. The only two members of the higher ranks of the legal profession which are particularly described are the two Serjeants who appear in *Bardell* v. *Pickwick*—Serjeants Buzfuz and Snubbin. The only judge who is particularly described is Mr. Justice Stareleigh; and of the Lord Chancellor in *Bleak House* only a slight description is given. I shall therefore begin from the bottom, and, in the first place, illustrate from Dickens's picture gallery the humbler satellites of the law, and the lawyers' clerks. In the second place I shall illustrate the various types of attorneys and solicitors. In the third place, I shall say something of the serjeants-at-law. Lastly I shall say a word of the barristers, king's counsel, and the judges.

Sheriff's officers have a considerable part to play in Dickens's novels. There is Neckett, the gruff officer from Coavinses, who came to arrest Harold Skimpole—"a person in a white great coat, with smooth hair upon his head, and not much of it, which he was wiping smoother, and making less of, with a pocket handkerchief," who "was never tired of watching," and would "sit upon a post at a street corner, eight or ten hours at a stretch, if he undertook to do it."* There is Namby, who arrested Mr. Pickwick,† "a man of about forty, with black hair and carefully combed whiskers. He was dressed in a particularly gorgeous manner with plenty of articles of jewelry about him—all about three sizes larger than those which are usually worn by gentlemen—a rough great coat to crown the whole. Into one pocket of this great-coat he thrust his left hand the moment he dis-

* *Bleak House,* chaps. vi and xv.

† *Pickwick,* chap. xl.

mounted, while from the other he drew forth, with his right, a very bright and glaring silk handkerchief, with which he whisked a speck or two of dust from his boots, and then, crumbling it in his hands, swaggered up the court." There is also Smouch, Namby's attendant—"a shabby looking man in a brown great coat shorn of divers buttons."

Snagsby, the kindly little law stationer with the vinegary wife, has a considerable part to play in *Bleak House*. He employed Nemo *alias* Captain Hawdon, round whom the plot of the whole story hinges. Nemo is one type of the hack copyist—the type which has sunk to this wretched life through vice or misfortune. Another type is Tony Jobling* —the flashy and extravagant clerk, whom Guppy befriends when he has been dismissed without a character. He takes up the trade of copying, under the name of Weevle, and occupies Nemo's wretched room. The office boy is portrayed in the unpleasant Smallweed—"something under fifteen and an old limb of the law," "a town made article of small stature and weazen features," whose great ambition is to become a Guppy.†

In Dickens's gallery of lawyers' clerks Guppy

* *Bleak House,* chap. xx. † *Ibid.*

is the most finished picture. He is a perfect type of cockney—with ambitions. His speech is modelled on the epistolary style of lawyers' letters, or on their spoken style in court; for his sole education has been in a lawyer's office. "What follows is without prejudice, miss," he says to Esther Summerson when he comes to propose to her; and the form of his proposal is a similar travesty of legal language—"Would you be so kind to allow me, as I might say, to file a declaration—to make an offer."* Yet he has considerable virtues. He must have been industrious and able, for Kenge and Carboy gave him his articles. He supports his vulgar and not very pleasant old mother, and, as we have seen, he befriended his friend Tony Jobling when he was down on his luck. Lowten, Perker's clerk, discovered by Pickwick presiding at a sing-song at the Magpie and Stump, at which sundry other lawyers' clerks were present, is the type of the efficient managing clerk. So too is Jackson, Dodson and Fogg's outdoor clerk, who served the subpœnas on Pickwick's friends, and later assisted at the arrest of Mrs. Bardell. So too was Wemmick, Jaggers's head clerk, with his little wooden cottage in the Walworth Road, got up to

* *Bleak House,* chap. ix.

imitate a fortified castle, and his collection of curiosities "of a felonious character."* Then, too, we have an account of Jaggers's other clerks—the clerk in appearance "something between a publican and a ratcatcher," and the "flabby terrier" of a clerk, both of whom were employed in getting evidence together; and the clerk who made fair copies of this evidence.†

The two most unpleasant of Dickens's clerks are Uriah Heep and Sally Brass. Uriah Heep, the humble, was a student of that encyclopædia of common procedure, *Tidd's Practice,* and the betrayer of his employer and benefactor.‡ Here is an early interview between David Copperfield and Uriah Heep: §

> Seeing a light in the little round office, and immediately feeling myself attracted towards Uriah Heep, who had a sort of fascination for me, I went in there instead. I found Uriah reading a great fat book, with such demonstrative attention, that his lank forefinger followed up every line as he read, and made clammy tracks along the page (or so I fully believed) like a snail.

* *Great Expectations,* chap. xxv.

† *Ibid.,* chap. xxiv.

‡ *David Copperfield,* chaps. xvi and lii.

§ *Ibid.,* chap. xvi.

"You are working late to-night, Uriah," says I.

"Yes, Master Copperfield," says Uriah.

As I was getting on the stool opposite, to talk to him more conveniently, I observed that he had not such a thing as a smile about him, and that he could only widen his mouth and make two hard creases down his cheeks, one on each side, to stand for one.

"I am not doing office-work, Master Copperfield," said Uriah.

"What work, then?" I asked.

"I am improving my legal knowledge, Master Copperfield," said Uriah. "I am going through Tidd's Practice. Oh, what a writer Mr. Tidd is, Master Copperfield!"

. . . "I suppose you are quite a great lawyer?" I said, after looking at him for some time.

"Me, Master Copperfield?" said Uriah. "Oh, no! I'm a very 'umble person."

Sally Brass, Dickens's one female lawyer, ran the business of her considerably more effeminate brother, Sampson Brass—"his clerk, assistant, housekeeper, secretary, confidential plotter, adviser, intriguer, and bill of costs increaser—a kind of amazon at common law."*

These types of lawyers' clerks belong to a van-

* *The Old Curiosity Shop,* chap. xxxii.

ished world. But it was once a real world. Mr. Jaques says:*

I recollect one ancient, a managing common law clerk, who could remember the green numbers of *Pickwick* coming out month by month, and who had many anecdotes of spunging houses and other vanished things mentioned therein. This veteran . . . had more than a touch of kinship with the Georgian law clerks whom Dickens knew. For example, he was a dungeon of learning as regards the practice, but he could never be prevailed upon to initiate a neophyte into its mysteries. Any appeal on the part of a would be disciple to share his toil at Judges' Chambers, then situate in the Rolls Gardens, and vulgarly known as the "Bear-garden," was diplomatically put aside; the fact being that, though my friend and his brother managing clerks were religiously absent from their employers' offices for some five hours every day, very little of this time was spent under the shadow of the Record Office. There was no occasion for these patriarchs to waste their energies upon squabbles before judges or masters; they of their ripe experience knew what orders the facts justified, and with a little give and take on both sides, the small blue oblong summonses of those days could be adorned with "consent endorsements," quite as effectual as those of the judicial officers them-

* *Charles Dickens in Chancery,* pp. 43-44.

selves. This excellent arrangement left ample time for social conversation and reasonable conviviality. I have been told—but I do not vouch for the fact—that the Rising Sun in Wych Street was the meeting place of the club . . . at which these choice spirits agreed upon their orders, and enjoyed the leisure to which they were so justly entitled.

We can imagine Mr. Lowten of Perker's, Mr. Guppy of Kenge and Carboy's, Mr. Jackson of Dodson and Fogg's, and Mr. Wemmick of Jaggers's meeting and conducting their business in this very way.

Attorneys were the practitioners in the common law courts: solicitors were practitioners in the Court of Chancery. They were originally different classes of legal practitioners; but, long before Dickens wrote, they had in effect become amalgamated. Generally all attorneys were solicitors and vice versa.

The attorney whose practice was of the highest class was Mr. Tulkinghorn, the legal adviser of Sir Leicester Dedlock, and of many other titled persons. Here is his portrait:*

* *Bleak House,* chap. ii.

Lawyers and Lawyers' Clerks

At Lady Dedlock's house in town, upon this muddy, murky afternoon, presents himself an old-fashioned old gentleman, attorney-at-law, and eke solicitor of the High Court of Chancery, who has the honour of acting as legal adviser of the Dedlocks, and has as many cast-iron boxes in his office with that name outside, as if the present baronet were the coin of the conjurer's trick, and were constantly being juggled through the whole set.

The old gentleman is rusty to look at, but is reputed to have made good thrift out of aristocratic marriage settlements and aristocratic wills, and to be very rich. He is surrounded by a mysterious halo of family confidences; of which he is known to be the silent depository. There are noble Mausoleums rooted for centuries in retired glades of parks, among the growing timber and the fern, which perhaps hold fewer noble secrets than walk abroad among men, shut up in the breast of Mr. Tulkinghorn. He is of what is called the old school—a phrase generally meaning any school that seems never to have been young—and wears knee breeches tied with ribbons, and gaiters or stockings. One peculiarity of his black clothes, and of his black stockings, be they silk or worsted, is, that they never shine. Mute, close, irresponsive to any glancing light, his dress is like himself. He never converses, when not professionally consulted. He is found sometimes, speechless but quite at home, at corners of dinner-tables in great country houses, and near doors of drawing-rooms, concerning which the fashionable intelligence is eloquent; where everybody knows him, and where half the Peerage stops to say, "How do you do Mr. Tulkinghorn?" He receives these salutations with gravity, and buries them along with the rest of his knowledge.

He was, as Lady Dedlock truly said, "the master of the mysteries of great houses." Sir F. Pollock, in his little book on the Land Laws,* has remarked how, by their system of strict settlement, English landowners had reproduced "something like the image of an archaic Aryan household"; and that when the observer notes "who is now the real possessor of the secrets of the estate, the real familiar spirit at whose bidding the magical powers of the settlement are called forth . . . he may peradventure dream that the disestablished Lar . . . is not dead but transformed, and lives embodied in the family solicitor." Tulkinghorn was the familiar spirit who looked after the fortunes of many noble families. And that he took this view of his functions can be seen from what he said to Lady Dedlock, when she spoke of "her secret." "It is no longer your secret. Excuse

*At pp. 115-117.

me, that is just the mistake. It is my secret in trust for Sir Leicester and the family."*

Perker†—"a little high dried man, with a dark squeezed up face, and small restless black eyes, that kept winking and twinkling on each side of his little inquisitive nose, as if they were playing a perpetual game of peep-bo with that feature"—Perker, was a solicitor with a good class general practice. Ellis of the firm of Ellis and Blackmore, whom Dickens served as a clerk, is said to have been his original. He acted as election agent for the Hon. Samuel Slumkey, the blue candidate at the Eatanswill election, which he secured for his principal by means of corrupt practices which were superior in intelligence to those of his rival.‡ He was on good terms with the rising members of all branches of the legal profession. At his dinner party, at which Mr. Lowten disturbed him to tell him that Mrs. Bardell had been arrested by Dodson and Fogg on a cognovit for costs and was in the Fleet prison, there were "Mr. Prosee, the eminent counsel, three solicitors, one commissioner of bankrupts, a special pleader from the Temple, a small-eyed peremptory young gentle-

* *Bleak House,* chap. xlviii. † *Pickwick,* chap. x.
‡ *Ibid.,* chap. xiii.

man his pupil, who had written a lively book about the law of demises . . . and several other eminent and distinguished personages."* No doubt he was a sound adviser in ordinary family business, and in cases which involved serious points of law. But he was no match for the Dodson and Fogg type of speculative action. Snubbin, who was no doubt a fine real property lawyer, was not the man to defend a breach of promise action, in which the facts were so much against the defendant. No doubt he might lead the court by the nose on a point of law; but Perker ought to have seen that that was not what was wanted in this class of case. Possibly, however, he could do no better. Dodson and Fogg had snapped up Buzfuz, and Snubbin may have been the best serjeant available. Anyhow, he is always ready to praise the smartness of that firm. " 'By Jove!' said Perker (when he heard of the arrest of Mrs. Bardell), 'those are the cleverest scamps I ever had anything to do with!' 'The sharpest practitioners *I* ever knew, sir,' observed Lowten. 'Sharp!' echoed Perker, 'there's no knowing where to have them.' 'Very true, sir, there is not,' replied Lowten; and then both master and man pondered for

* *Pickwick,* chap. xlvii.

a few seconds, with animated countenances, as if they were reflecting upon one of the most beautiful and ingenious discoveries that the intellect of man had ever made."* And really it was an unprecedented situation—it was not often that a firm of solicitors could succeed in taking in execution for costs both the plaintiff and the defendant in the action. To Pickwick, Perker talked about the possibility of an indictment for conspiracy—but admitted that Dodson and Fogg were too clever to have laid themselves open to that; and could only hold out hopes that one day they would overreach themselves, and crash. His management of Pickwick is as admirable as his management of Pickwick's case was stupid. On the whole he is the most likable of all the attorneys in Dickens.

There is no doubt at all what Dickens thought of the firm of Dodson and Fogg, and what he wished his readers to think. They were unpleasant in appearance. Fogg "was an elderly, pimply faced, vegetable diet sort of man, in a black coat, dark mixture trousers, and small black gaiters; a kind of being who seemed to be an essential part of the desk at which he was writing, and to have as much thought or sentiment."† Dodson was "a

* *Pickwick,* chap. xlvii.

† *Ibid.,* chap. xx.

plump, portly, stern looking man with a loud voice."* Their practice was of the sharpest, but clever enough to keep inside the line. The case of Ramsay†—a poor man whose offer to pay his debt and costs was refused because it was falsely stated that further costs had been incurred—is a very bad one; and, if Mrs. Bardell's confession is to be believed, they were guilty of something very like maintenance in getting her to bring her action. On the other hand their conduct of Mrs. Bardell's case was admirable; and they quite outclassed Perker. In fact it has been suggested by some legal critics, who have undertaken their defence,‡ that, not only is their professional conduct regular, but that they acted with restraint in not suing Pickwick for his abuse of them at sundry interviews. As to that, I think it may be said that parts of their professional conduct were very much on the line; and that their treatment of Pickwick, in view both of Mrs. Bardell's confession, and the obstinacy of Pickwick's character, shows that they were clever enough to come to the right conclusion that discretion was the better part of valor.

* *Pickwick,* chap. xx. † *Ibid.*

‡ See Sir Frank Lockwood, *Law and Lawyers of Pickwick;* P. Fitzgerald, *Bardell* v. *Pickwick.*

They were also clever enough to avoid the crash which Perker, to comfort Pickwick, prophesied for them; for we read in the last chapter that they were still in business, "from which they realize a large income, and in which they are universally considered among the sharpest of the sharp."

In *The Battle of Life** we are introduced to a firm of country solicitors—Messrs. Snitchey and Craggs. Snitchey was evidently a real property lawyer, for he looks at a landscape with the eye of a conveyancer:

> "Here's a smiling country once overrun by soldiers —trespassers every man of 'em—and laid waste by fire and sword. But take this smiling country as it stands. Think of the laws appertaining to real property; to the bequest and devise of real property; to the mortgage and redemption of real property; to leasehold, freehold, and copyhold estate; think," said Mr. Snitchey, with such great emotion that he actually smacked his lips, "of the complicated laws relating to title and proof of title, with all the contradictory precedents and numerous acts of parliament connected with them; think of the infinite number of ingenious and interminable chancery suits, to which this pleasant prospect may give rise; and acknowledge, Dr. Jeddler,

* Printed in the volume of *Christmas Books*.

that there is a green spot in the scheme about us! I believe," said Mr. Snitchey, looking at his partner, "that I speak for Self and Craggs?"

The attorney who devotes himself to criminal practice is painted for us in *Great Expectations.* A wonderful picture is drawn of Jaggers and his high-handed dealings with his clients, and with magistrates and other officers of the law. Here is a picture of his dealings with his clients: *

I saw Mr. Jaggers coming across the road towards me. All the others who were waiting, saw him at the same time, and there was quite a rush at him. Mr. Jaggers, putting a hand on my shoulder and walking me on at his side without saying anything to me, addressed himself to his followers.

First, he took the two secret men.

"Now, I have nothing to say to *you,*" said Mr. Jaggers, throwing his finger at them. "I want to know no more than I know. As to the result, it's a toss-up. I told you from the first it was a toss-up. Have you paid Wemmick?"

"We made the money up this morning, sir," said one of the men, submissively, while the other perused Mr. Jaggers's face.

"I don't ask you when you made it up, or where, or

* *Great Expectations,* chap. xx.

whether you made it up at all. Has Wemmick got it?"

"Yes, sir," said both the men together.

"Very well; then you may go. Now, I won't have it!" said Mr. Jaggers, waving his hand at them to put them behind him. "If you say a word to me, I'll throw up the case."

"We thought, Mr. Jaggers——" one of the men began, pulling off his hat.

"That's what I told you not to do," said Mr. Jaggers. "*You* thought! I think for you; that's enough for you. If I want you, I know where to find you; I don't want you to find me. Now I won't have it. I won't hear a word."

The two men looked at one another as Mr. Jaggers waved them behind again, and humbly fell back and were heard no more.

"And now *you!*" said Mr. Jaggers, suddenly stopping, and turning on the two women with the shawls, from whom the three men had meekly separated—"Oh! Amelia, is it?"

"Yes, Mr. Jaggers."

"And do you remember," retorted Mr. Jaggers, "that but for me you wouldn't be here and couldn't be here?"

"Oh yes, sir!" exclaimed both women together. "Lord bless you, sir, well we knows that!"

"Then why," said Mr. Jaggers, "do you come here?"

"My Bill, sir?" the crying woman pleaded.

"Now, I tell you what!" said Mr. Jaggers. "Once for all. If you don't know that your Bill's in good hands, I know it. And if you come here, bothering about your Bill, I'll make an example of both your Bill and you, and let him slip through my fingers. Have you paid Wemmick?"

"Oh yes, sir! Every farden."

"Very well. Then you have done all you have got to do. Say another word—one single word—and Wemmick shall give you your money back."

This terrible threat caused the two women to fall off immediately. No one remained now but the excitable Jew, who had already raised the skirts of Mr. Jaggers's coat to his lips several times.

"I don't know this man?" said Mr. Jaggers, in the most devastating strain. "What does this fellow want?"

"Ma thear Mithter Jaggerth. Hown brother to Habraham Latharuth!"

"Who's he?" said Mr. Jaggers. "Let go of my coat."

The suitor, kissing the hem of the garment again before relinquishing it, replied, "Habraham Latharuth, on thuthpithion of plate."

"You're too late," said Mr. Jaggers. "I am over the way."

"Holy father, Mithter Jaggerth!" cried my excitable acquaintance, turning white, "don't thay you're again Habraham Latharuth!"

"I am," said Mr. Jaggers, "and there's an end of it. Get out of the way."

"Mithter Jaggerth! Half a moment! My hown cuthen'th gone to Mithter Wemmick at thith prethenth minute to hoffer him hany termth. Mithter Jaggerth! Half a quarter of a moment! If you'd have the condethenthun to be bought off from the t'other thide—at any thuperior prithe!—money no object!—Mithter Jaggerth—Mithter—!"

My guardian threw his supplicant off with supreme indifference, and left him dancing on the pavement as if it were red-hot.

Here is a picture of his demeanor in court:*

We dived into the City, and came up in a crowded police-court, where a blood-relation (in the murderous sense) of the deceased with the fanciful taste in brooches, was standing at the bar, uncomfortably chewing something; while my guardian had a woman under examination or cross-examination—I don't know which—and was striking her, and the bench, and everybody with awe. If anybody, of whatsoever degree, said a word that he didn't approve of, he instantly required to have it "taken down." If anybody wouldn't make an admission, he said, "I'll have it out of you!" and if anybody made an admission, he said, "Now I have got you!" The magistrates shivered

* *Great Expectations,* chap. xxiv.

under a single bite of his finger. Thieves and thief-takers hung in dread rapture on his words, and shrank when a hair of his eyebrows turned in their direction. Which side he was on I couldn't make out, for he seemed to me to be grinding the whole place in a mill; I only know that when I stole out on tiptoe he was not on the side of the bench; for he was making the legs of the old gentleman who presided quite convulsive under the table, by his denunciations of his conduct as the representative of British law and justice in that chair that day.

We can sympathise with the despair of Abraham Lazarus when he heard that Jaggers was retained for the crown.*

Digressing for a moment from the attorneys, to the magistrates before whom attorneys of the type of Jaggers practised, we should notice that Fang, the magistrate before whom Oliver Twist was brought up, was a caricature of the bad tempered Mr. Laing, who presided at the Hatton Garden Police Court. As a writer in the *Law Times* has recently pointed out,† Fang was prepared to gerrymander the charge in order to give himself jurisdiction. Oliver Twist was charged with the

* *Great Expectations,* chap. xx.
† *Law Times,* vol. 117, p. 308.

felony of picking the pocket of Mr. Brownlow. Fang dealt with the case summarily by treating it as loitering with intent to commit a felony—an offence under the Vagrancy Act—instead of committing Oliver Twist to be tried for felony.

Returning to the attorneys and descending in the scale, we come to Solomon Pell, the seedy practitioner in the Insolvent Court, and the friend, according to his own account, of a Lord Chancellor. These practitioners, Dickens tells us, were the great curiosities of that court; and of them in general, and of Solomon Pell in particular, we have the following description.*

But the attorneys, who sit at a large bare table below the Commissioners, are, after all, the greatest curiosities. The professional establishment of the more opulent of these gentlemen, consists of a blue bag and a boy: generally a youth of the Jewish persuasion. They have no fixed offices, their legal business being transacted in the parlours of public-houses, or the yards of prisons: whither they repair in crowds, and canvass for customers after the manner of omnibus cads. They are of a greasy and mildewed appearance; and if they can be said to have any vices at all, perhaps drinking and cheating are the most conspicuous

* *Pickwick,* chap. xliii.

among them. Their residences are usually on the outskirts of "the Rules," chiefly lying within a circle of one mile from the obelisk in St. George's Fields. Their looks are not prepossessing, and their manners are peculiar.

Mr. Solomon Pell, one of this learned body, was a fat flabby pale man, in a surtout which looked green one minute and brown the next: with a velvet collar of the same cameleon tints. His forehead was narrow, his face wide, his head large, and his nose all on one side, as if Nature indignant with the propensities she observed in him in his birth, had given it an angry tweak which it had never recovered. Being short-necked and asthmatic, however, he respired principally through this feature; so, perhaps, what it wanted in ornament, it made up in usefulness.

The most repulsive of all the attorneys is Sampson Brass of Bevis Marks in the City of London—a cowardly criminal—well matched with his principal client, Daniel Quilp.*

He was a tall, meagre man, with a nose like a wen, a protruding forehead, retreating eyes, and hair of a deep red. He wore a long black surtout reaching nearly to his ankles, short black trousers, high shoes, and cotton stockings of a bluish grey. He had a cringing

* *Old Curiosity Shop,* chap. xi.

manner, but a very harsh voice; and his blandest smiles were so extremely forbidding, that to have had his company under the least repulsive circumstances, one would have wished him to be out of temper that he might only scowl.

The proctors of Doctors' Commons are represented by Spenlow and Jorkins. Spenlow was "a little light-haired gentleman, with undeniable boots, and the stiffest of white cravats and shirt collars. He was buttoned up mighty trim and tight, and must have taken a great deal of pains with his whiskers, which were accurately curled."* Jorkins, his partner, whom he always represented as "an obdurate and ruthless man," when it was necessary to refuse inconvenient requests, was really "a mild man of a heavy temperament whose place in the business was to keep himself in the background."†

I pass now to the higher branches of the legal profession.

The order of the serjeants at law‡ was abolished by the Judicature Act of 1873, which came into

* *David Copperfield,* chap. xxiii.

† *Ibid.*

‡ See generally Pulling, *The Order of the Coif;* Holdsworth, *Hist. Engl. Law* (3d ed.), II, 485-492; VI, 477-478.

operation in 1875, and the last surviving serjeant at law—Lord Lindley—died in 1921 at the age of 93. In 1877 Serjeant's Inn was sold, and partitioned out among the surviving serjeants. It has now been pulled down, and "like Faringdon's Inn, New Inn, and Clement's Inn, it has joined the ghosts of the law."* In the Middle Ages the serjeants belonged to an order which took rank as the highest in the legal profession; and from them the king selected certain king's serjeants to represent him in his courts. They were almost on an equality with the judges. In fact they and the judges were brothers of one order; and they addressed one another as such. The judges were appointed exclusively from their ranks; and they lodged together at the Serjeant's Inn. Their gradual decline began in the latter part of the sixteenth century. The rule that the judges were appointed exclusively from their order then began to be evaded, by making the man, whom it was wished to raise to the bench, a serjeant *pro forma;* and this practice continued till the Judicature Acts. Field and Lindley in 1875 were the last two lawyers to be made serjeants as a preliminary to

* *Law Quarterly Review,* XXXV, 264.

becoming judges.* In fact their position as the leaders of the bar was being undermined by the rise in importance of the attorney and solicitor-general, who replaced the king's serjeants, and by the growth of the new order of king's counsel. The king's counsel were originally what the name implies—the advisers of the king. They were assistants employed by the attorney and solicitor-general. But in the course of the seventeenth century they became a regular order of counsel, who took rank above the serjeants. In fact, the serjeants were essentially a mediæval order; and the king's serjeants were mediæval officials. Like many other mediæval institutions, they were obliged to give place to new institutions, better adapted to the needs of the modern state.

But one privilege they retained down to 1846.† They had the monopoly of audience as pleaders at the Common Pleas Bar. The crown had attempted to abolish this monopoly in 1834; but the attack was successfully resisted; so that it was necessary for Mrs. Bardell and Mr. Pickwick to retain serjeants to represent them.

The original of Serjeant Buzfuz, Mrs. Bardell's

* *Law Quarterly Review,* XXXV, 275.

† 9 & 10 Victoria, c. 54.

counsel, was Mr. Serjeant Bompas, who was made a serjeant in 1827. He is represented as possessing a "fat body and a red face"; and he was certainly the man to brief for a case like Mrs. Bardell's. Both his speech to the jury,* and his examinations of the witnesses were masterly. His famous treatment of the only letters which had passed between the plaintiff and defendant was calculated to impress the jury—having regard to the admissions made by witnesses who were admittedly friends of the defendant. It is well known that Dickens got his idea for this part of the serjeant's speech from a contemporary *cause celebre*—the action brought by Mr. Norton against Lord Melbourne for criminal conversation.† Mr. Theobold Mathew has printed part of Sir William Follett's speech for the plaintiff in that action.‡ Sir William, after explaining that all the letters except three had disappeared, said,

> These three notes, which have since been found, relate only to his hours of calling on Mrs. Norton,

* Mr. Atlay, *Victorian Chancellors,* II, 163 n. 2, says, "I have always believed that the speech of Serjeant Buzfuz was largely indebted to the eloquence of Charles Phillips on behalf of the plaintiff in *Guthrie* v. *Sterne,* an Irish case printed in 1822."

† See *ibid.,* II, 161-164.

‡ *Law Quarterly Review,* XXXIV, 325-326.

nothing more; but there is something in the style even of these trivial notes to lead at least to something like suspicion. Here is one of them: "I will call about ½ past 4 or 5 o'clock. Yours, Melbourne." There is no regular beginning of the letters; they don't commence with "My dear Mrs. Norton," or anything of that sort, as is usual in this country when a gentleman writes to a lady. Here is another . . . "How are you?" Again there is no beginning, as you see. "How are you? I shall not be able to call to-day, but probably shall to-morrow. Yours, &c., Melbourne." This is not the note of a gentleman to a lady with whom he may be acquainted. The third runs: "There is no house to-day. I shall call after the levée, about 4 or ½ past. If you wish it later let me know. I shall then explain to you about going to Vauxhall. Yours, &c., Melbourne" . . . They seem to import much more than the words convey. They are written cautiously, I admit—there is no profession of love in them, they are not love-letters, but they are not written in the ordinary style of correspondence usually adopted . . . between intimate friends.

Now compare this with Serjeant Buzfuz's speech:*

And now, gentlemen, but one word more. Two letters have passed between these parties, letters which

* *Pickwick,* chap. xxxiv.

are admitted to be in the handwriting of the defendant, and which speak volumes indeed. These letters, too, bespeak the character of the man. They are not open, fervent, eloquent epistles, breathing nothing but the language of affectionate attachment. They are covert, sly, underhanded communications, but, fortunately, far more conclusive than if couched in the most glowing language and the most poetic imagery—letters that must be viewed with a cautious and suspicious eye—letters that were evidently intended at the time, by Pickwick, to mislead and delude any third parties into whose hands they might fall. Let me read the first:—"Garraway's, twelve o'clock—Dear Mrs. B.—Chops and Tomato sauce. Yours, Pickwick!" Gentlemen, what does this mean? Chops and Tomato sauce. Yours, Pickwick! Chops! Gracious heavens! and Tomato sauce! Gentlemen, is the happiness of a sensitive and confiding female to be trifled away by such shallow artifices as these? The next has no date whatever, which is in itself suspicious. "Dear Mrs. B., I shall not be at home till to-morrow. Slow coach." And then follows this very remarkable expression: "Don't trouble yourself about the warming-pan." The warming-pan! Why, gentlemen, who *does* trouble himself about a warming-pan? When was the peace of mind of a man or woman broken or disturbed by a warming-pan, which is in itself a harmless, a useful, and I will add, gentlemen, a comforting article of domestic furniture? Why is Mrs. Bardell so earnestly entreated not to agitate herself about this warming-pan, unless (as is no doubt the case) it is a mere cover for hidden fire —a mere substitute for some endearing word or promise, agreeably to a preconcerted system of correspondence, artfully contrived by Pickwick with a view to his contemplated desertion, and which I am not in a condition to explain? And what does this allusion to the slow coach mean?

Serjeant Snubbin is described* as

a lantern-faced, sallow-complexioned man, of about five-and-forty, or—as the novels say—he might be fifty. He had that dull-looking boiled eye which is often to be seen in the heads of people who have applied themselves during many years to a weary and laborious course of study; and which would have been sufficient, without the additional eye-glass which dangled from a broad black riband round his neck, to warn a stranger that he was very near-sighted. His hair was thin and weak, which was partly attributable to his having never devoted much time to its arrangement, and partly to his having worn for five-and-twenty years the forensic wig which hung on a block beside him. The marks of hair-powder on his coat-collar, and the ill-washed and worse tied white neckerchief round his throat, showed that he had not found leisure since he

* *Pickwick,* chap. xxxi.

left the court to make any alteration in his dress: while the slovenly style of the remainder of his costume warranted the inference that his personal appearance would not have been very much improved if he had.

He was not without his merits as an advocate: for we are told that in a long and emphatic address he did the best he could for Mr. Pickwick. But no doubt he would have been more at home arguing a point of real property law. That was what really interested him; for, when Pickwick visited his chambers, and he had successfully got rid of him by handing him over to Phunky, he at once immersed himself in the case before him "which arose out of an interminable law suit, originating in the act of an individual, deceased a century or so ago, who had stopped up a pathway leading from some place which nobody ever came from, to some other place which nobody ever went to."*

Dickens has little to say of the ordinary barrister. The Bar in general is described in the party given by Mr. Merdle in *Little Dorrit;*† and it is said that Fitzroy Kelly was the original.‡

* *Pickwick,* chap. xxxi. † Bk. I, chap. xxi.
‡ Atlay, *Victorian Chancellors,* II, 101.

Bar, with his little insinuating Jury droop, and fingering his persuasive double eye-glass, hoped he might be excused if he mentioned to one of the greatest converters of the root of all evil into the root of all good, who had for a long time reflected a shining lustre on the annals even of our commercial country—if he mentioned, disinterestedly, and as what we lawyers called in our pedantic way, amicus curiæ, a fact that had come by accident within his knowledge. He had been required to look over the title of a very considerable estate in one of the eastern counties—lying, in fact, for Mr. Merdle knew we lawyers loved to be particular, on the borders of two of the eastern counties. Now the title was perfectly sound, and the estate was to be purchased by one who had the command of—Money (Jury droop and persuasive eye-glass), on remarkably advantageous terms. This had come to Bar's knowledge only that day, and it had occurred to him, "I shall have the honour of dining with my esteemed friend Mr. Merdle this evening, and, strictly between ourselves, I will mention the opportunity." Such a purchase would involve not only great legitimate political influence, but some half-dozen church presentations of considerable annual value. Now that Mr. Merdle was already at no loss to discover means of occupying even his capital, and of fully employing even his active and vigorous intellect, Bar well knew: but he would venture to suggest that the question arose in his mind, whether one who had deservedly gained so high a position and so European a reputation did not owe it—we would not say to himself, but we would say to Society, to possess himself of such influences as these; and to exercise them—we would not say for his own, or for his party's, but we would say for Society's—benefit.

In *A Tale of Two Cities* we have pictures of Mr. Stryver, the common law pleader, and his clever devil, Sydney Carton.*

A favourite at the Old Bailey, and eke at the Sessions, Mr. Stryver had begun cautiously to hew away the lower staves of the ladder on which he mounted. Sessions and Old Bailey had now to summon their favourite, specially, to their longing arms; and shouldering itself towards the visage of the Lord Chief Justice in the Court of King's Bench, the florid countenance of Mr. Stryver might be daily seen, bursting out of the bed of wigs, like a great sunflower pushing its way at the sun from among a rank gardenfull of flaring companions.

It had once been noted at the Bar, that while Mr. Stryver was a glib man, and an unscrupulous, and a ready, and a bold, he had not that faculty of extracting the essence from a heap of statements, which is among the most striking and necessary of the advocate's ac-

* Bk. II, chap. v.

complishments. But a remarkable improvement came upon him as to this. The more business he got, the greater his power seemed to grow of getting at its pith and marrow; and however late at night he sat carousing with Sydney Carton, he always had his points at his fingers' ends in the morning.

Sydney Carton, idlest and most unpromising of men, was Stryver's great ally. What the two drank together, between Hilary Term and Michaelmas, might have floated a king's ship. Stryver never had a case in hand, anywhere, but Carton was there, with his hands in his pockets, staring at the ceiling of the court; they went the same Circuit, and even there they prolonged their usual orgies late into the night, and Carton was rumoured to be seen at broad day, going home stealthily and unsteadily to his lodgings, like a dissipated cat. At last, it began to get about, among such as were interested in the matter, that although Sydney Carton would never be a lion, he was an amazingly good jackal, and that he rendered suit and service to Stryver in that humble capacity.

Stryver's cross-examination in the trial scene in *A Tale of Two Cities** is said to have been suggested by Wetherall's cross-examination of Castle in the trials for treason arising out of the Spa Fields riots in 1816.† The two members of the

* Bk. II, chap. iii. † Atlay, *Victorian Chancellors,* I, 18.

junior bar in *Bardell* v. *Pickwick* were Skimpin and Phunky. It has been suggested that Skimpin, Buzfuz's junior, and a very able young man, was one Wilkins, who later became a serjeant.* But, as Mr. Theobald Mathew has said, both Skimpin and Phunky are only types of men who exist to-day in the flesh in large numbers.† The only king's counsel of whom there is any description is Mr. Tangle, K.C., who is eloquently addressing the court in the first chapter of *Bleak House,* and whose speech was not finished when the court arose.

The only portrait of a judge is Stareleigh, J.—a thin disguise for Gaselee, J.—who tried the case of *Bardell* v. *Pickwick.* Gaselee became a judge in 1824. He is said by Foss to have been "a painstaking and upright judge";‡ but it is noteworthy that he resigned in the Hilary Term, 1837—shortly after the appearance of the trial scene in *Pickwick.* The physical likeness between him and Stareleigh was as marked as the resemblance of the name. He

* P. Fitzgerald, *Bardell* v. *Pickwick,* p. 61; for further information as to Wilkins see Atlay, *Victorian Chancellors,* I, 430.

† *Law Quarterly Review,* XXXIV, 324.

‡ Foss, *Judges,* IX, 91.

was a most particularly short man, and so fat, that he seemed all face and waistcoat. He rolled in, upon two little turned legs, and having bobbed gravely to the bar, who bobbed gravely to him, put his little legs underneath his table, and his little three-cornered hat upon it; and when Mr. Justice Stareleigh had done this, all you could see of him was two queer little eyes, one broad pink face, and somewhere about half of a big and very comical-looking wig.*

And probably the intellectual likeness was as striking. He is credited with the qualities of irritability, deafness, and inability to produce an adequate summing up. In his younger days, at any rate, he had no illusions as to his professional chances. He is said to have betted a friend 100 to 1 that he would never reach the bench—which he duly paid to the son of his deceased friend when he became a judge.†

Of Lord Lyndhurst, the only chancellor in whose court Dickens reported, we have a sketch in the third chapter of *Bleak House*. As Mr. Atlay has said in his able and interesting *Lives of the Victorian Chancellors*,‡ "the figure of Lord Lynd-

* *Pickwick*, chap. xxxiv.

† *Law Quarterly Review*, XXXIV, 323.

‡ I, 143.

hurst shines out even through the moral and material fog of *Jarndyce* v. *Jarndyce*." Here is Dickens's description:

> Presently he rose courteously . . . and then he spoke for a minute or two with Richard Carstone; not seated, but standing, and altogether with more ease and less ceremony—as if he still knew, though he *was* Lord Chancellor, how to go straight to the candour of a boy.
>
> "Very well!" said his lordship aloud. "I shall make the order. Mr. Jarndyce of Bleak House has chosen, so far as I may judge," and this was when he looked at me, "a very good companion for the young lady, and the arrangement altogether seems the best of which the circumstances admit."
>
> He dismissed us pleasantly, and we all went out, very much obliged to him for being so affable and polite; by which he had certainly lost no dignity, but seemed to us to have gained some.

I must now pass from the lawyers to the system which they administered; and first I shall deal with *Bleak House* and the procedure of the Court of Chancery.

III.

Bleak House and the Procedure of the Court of Chancery.

IF it be true that the Lord Chancellor described in the third chapter of *Bleak House* is Lord Lyndhurst, the time at which the action of the story takes place must be taken to be in or about 1827, when he was made Chancellor in succession to Lord Eldon. That was the very worst period of the Court of Chancery. The report of the first Chancery Commission, which had been published in the preceding year, had revealed a monstrous state of affairs, and as yet the Legislature had not begun the long task of applying a remedy. Obviously, in considering the contribution which *Bleak House* makes to the history of the Court of Chancery, we must keep this date in mind; and we must distinguish between this date, and the date when the story was written. The story appeared in parts between March, 1852, and September, 1853—at a time when considerable reforms had already been made, and on the eve of a very much larger instalment of reform.

The attention of Dickens had been directed to

the Court of Chancery by the fact that in 1844 he had, as we have seen, been the plaintiff in five Chancery actions to restrain breaches of copyright. He had been victorious; but he had failed to recover the costs from the defendants; and the small glimpse which he had had of the working of the court, seems to have had an effect on his mind similar to the effect which it had on the mind of Bentham. Two years later he was advised to take further proceedings for other piracies. He wrote, "My feeling is the feeling common, I suppose, to three-fourths of the reflecting part of the community in our happiest of all possible countries, and that is, that it is better to suffer a great wrong than to have recourse to the much greater wrong of the law. I shall not easily forget the expense and anxiety, and horrible injustice of the *Carol* case, wherein, in asserting the plainest right on earth, I was really treated as if I were the robber, instead of the robbed. I know of nothing that *could* come, even of a successful action, which would be worth the mental trouble and disturbance it would cost."*

In 1850 he wrote an article in *Household Words* on "The Martyrs of Chancery," which dealt with

* Forster, *Life of Dickens,* II, 75-76.

the hopeless lot of persons committed for contempt of court, who were forgotten, and left to die in prison. Sir Edward Sugden (the future Lord St. Leonards) had no difficulty in showing that that particular abuse was then a thing of the past.* Dickens was mistaken when he alleged in 1850 that this was at that date an existing abuse. But, assuming that the action of the story of *Bleak House* takes place in 1827, I do not think that it can be alleged that his statements of fact in that book are erroneous. He says in his Preface that "everything set forth in these pages concerning the Court of Chancery is substantially true and within the truth." That is not wholly true if he meant, as I think he did, to refer to the date when the book was written—though much of it was then still true. It would have been wholly true if he had meant to refer to the date of the action of the story. In fact, I am sure that it would be possible to produce an edition of *Bleak House,* in which all Dickens's statements could be verified by the statements of the witnesses who gave evidence before the Chancery Commission, which reported in 1826.

Let us look at the thing to be examined. The

* Atlay, *Victorian Chancellors,* II, 35-37.

following extract from my history summarizes what the Chancery Commissioners of 1850 found to be then the course of the procedure of the court:*

The plaintiff began his suit by addressing a bill to the chancellor, praying process against the defendant to compel him to appear and put in an answer. The bill asked for relief, and required the defendant to make discovery, i.e. to give on oath an answer to the matters stated and the interrogatories contained in the bill. The bill was then engrossed on parchment and filed with the proper officer of the court. A subpœna then issued, requiring the defendant to appear and answer. This subpœna contained no intimation of the object of the suit. The defendant must then appear and get an office copy of the bill. Having obtained this copy, the defendant must decide whether he would demur or plead or answer. He might demur, either on the substantial ground that no case had been made out for the interference of the court, or by reason of a technical objection to the form of the bill. A plea was generally a statement of matters not appearing on the face of the bill, which showed a reason why the suit should be either barred or delayed. The answer, which was generally given on oath, both answered the plaintiff's interrogatories contained in the bill and set out other

* Holdsworth, *Hist. Engl. Law,* IX, 340-342.

facts essential to the defendant's defence. Unless the defendant lived within twenty miles of London, a special commission issued to take the answer. This involved office fees, charges by the London solicitor who took it out, and fees to the Commissioners for swearing. There were frequent applications to a master for more time to answer, and appeals from his decision to the court. Omission to put in an answer in the proper time was punished by attachment; and, if the defendant was attached, all applications for time must be made to the court. After a sufficient answer was filed, a motion was made by the plaintiff for the production of documents in the defendant's possession. This order was also the occasion of considerable expense. It often happened that the answer of the defendant made it necessary for the plaintiff to amend his bill, in order either to traverse the facts stated in the answer, or to introduce new facts. Further answers were then called for; and the case could then either be heard on these answers, or the plaintiff could put in a formal replication denying the answers. The pleadings being thus at an end, the next step was to lay them before counsel to advise on the evidence, and to prepare interrogatories for the examination of witnesses. On these interrogatories the witnesses were examined in private, none of the parties or their agents being present. As the interrogatories were framed by counsel without knowing what witnesses would be forthcoming, or what answers they would give, it was necessary to frame questions to meet many possible contingencies. It is obvious that in these circumstances, no effective cross-examination was possible, so that it was seldom resorted to. It was necessary to issue a special commission to take the evidence of witnesses in the country—a process which was at once expensive and slow. When all the evidence had been taken it was published; and the parties could get copies on payment of fees. The case was then ripe for hearing; but it could be delayed by motions to suppress depositions, or to issue another commission to take further evidence. When the case was set down for hearing, there were often further delays, by reason of objections taken on account of the misjoinder of a party, or non-joinder of necessary parties, or the death of a party, or the emerging of new facts. This was the occasion of bills of revivor or supplement, which often meant that the same tedious course of procedure must be started anew. Even if all these defects were cured, it was often still not possible for the court to pronounce a final judgment unless it was a judgment dismissing the bill. It was often necessary to send the case to a master to take accounts or to make inquiries. Again, if at the hearing a question of law arose, a special case might be sent to a court of law, or the court might require a plaintiff to test his legal right by bringing an action at law. Moreover, if on the depositions the court could not come to a clear conclusion as to the facts, it might direct that an issue should be tried by a jury in a court of common law. Even if final judgment were at length given, many more delays could be interposed by a petition for rehearing or an appeal.

The physical fog amidst which *Bleak House* opens, which is so aptly made to typify the moral fog which enveloped the procedure of the Court of Chancery, is I think the finest piece of descriptive writing in the whole of Dickens's works. This moral fog had been produced by a variety of causes, operating through centuries; and its density had made the court the most crying abuse of an age in which there were many abuses. Let us glance rapidly at some of its causes. They can, I think, be grouped under four heads.

In the first place, the officers of the court were wholly inadequate to cope with its business. In its main outlines the official machinery was mediæval. No doubt it had been added to from time to time; but it had been added to piecemeal by the process of allowing the original officials to employ deputies. The original officials gathered in the fees which grew as the business of the court expanded;

and the work was done by underpaid deputies.* In the second place, even if its official machinery had been adequate, its practice had become so technical, and its procedure had become so slow, that the length of time taken to decide even uncontested cases amounted to a denial of justice. This was due to the fact that, for centuries, there had been no adequate supervision either of the officials, or of the procedural rules of the court. Both officials and practitioners went their own way, and disregarded inconvenient statutes† and orders made by the Chancellor. Indeed, it was admitted that a contrary course of practice might deprive these orders of their legal effect.‡ In the third place, even if the orders of the Chancellors had been carried out, there were still left a large crop of survivals of older rules of practice, which increased the delay and expense—survivals which it was impossible to get rid of, because officials had a vested interest in their maintenance. I will give two examples out of many. (i) At one time

* See Holdsworth, *Hist. Engl. Law* (3d ed.), I, 416-423, 424-428, 439-442.

† See Spence, *Equitable Jurisdiction,* I, 401, n. (*d*) for the manner in which a statute of James I was disregarded.

‡ See *Boehm* v. *De Tastet* (1813), 1 V. and B at p. 327 *per* Lord Eldon, cited Holdsworth, *Hist. Engl. Law,* IX, 343 n. 4.

the parties had been represented by the clerks of the court. Later they employed their own solicitors. But the fees to the clerks of the court remained.* (ii) To conserve the profits of the officials of the court, the parties were made to purchase from them office copies of documents which, in the eighteenth century, were wholly useless.† Fourthly and lastly, the court had bound itself by the rigid rule that, if it acted at all, it must assume entire control. It would not, for instance, decide a single doubtful point connected with the administration of an estate, without administering the whole estate. All the weary procedure must be gone through; and, if as was likely, new parties were born there was a lengthy procedure to add the necessary parties.‡ Gibbon's comment on the condition of Roman law in the time of Justinian applies exactly to the procedure of the Court of Chancery in 1827—it was "a mysterious science and a profitable trade," and, "the innate perplexity of the study was involved in tenfold darkness by the private industry of the practitioners."§

* Holdsworth, *Hist. Engl. Law,* IX, 370.

† *Ibid.,* pp. 361-362; cp. *ibid.* (3d ed.), I, 426, 441.

‡ *Ibid.,* pp. 347-348.

§ *Decline and Fall of the Roman Empire,* chap. xliv.

The result was the case of *Jarndyce* v. *Jarndyce* —the greatest Chancery suit, as Mr. Kenge explained, ever known. If we remember that, when, between 1824 and 1826, the court was put on its trial before the first Chancery Commission, witnesses were found to defend all parts of its procedure, we can see that the views as to that case, attributed to Mr. Kenge, were by no means outrageous.*

"Not heard of Jarndyce—the greatest of Chancery suits known? Not of Jarndyce and Jarndyce—the—a —in itself a monument of Chancery practice. In which (I would say) every difficulty, every contingency, every masterly fiction, every form of procedure known in that court, is represented over and over again? It is a cause that could not exist, out of this free and great country. I should say that the aggregate of costs in Jarndyce and Jarndyce amounts at the present hour to from *six-ty* to *seven-ty thousand pounds!*" said Mr. Kenge, leaning back in his chair.

On the other hand the view of the ordinary suitor is well represented by John Jarndyce: †

"A certain Jarndyce, in an evil hour, made a great fortune, and made a great Will. In the question how

* *Bleak House,* chap. iii. † *Ibid.,* chap. viii.

the trusts under that Will are to be administered, the fortune left by the Will is squandered away; the legatees under the Will are reduced to such a miserable condition that they would be sufficiently punished, if they had committed an enormous crime in having money left them; and the Will itself is made a dead letter. All through the deplorable cause, everything that everybody in it, except one man, knows already, is referred to that only one man who don't know it, to find out—all through the deplorable cause, everybody must have copies, over and over again, of everything that has accumulated about it in the way of cartloads of papers (or must pay for them without having them, which is the usual course, for nobody wants them); and must go down the middle and up again, through such an infernal country-dance of costs and fees and nonsense and corruption, as was never dreamed of in the wildest visions of a Witch's Sabbath. Equity sends questions to Law, Law sends questions back to Equity; Law finds it can't do this, Equity finds it can't do that; neither can so much as say it can't do anything, without this solicitor instructing and this counsel appearing for A, and that solicitor instructing and that counsel appearing for B; and so on through the whole alphabet, like the history of the Apple Pie. And thus, through years and years, and lives and lives, everything goes on, constantly beginning over and over again, and nothing ever ends. And we can't get out of the suit on any terms, for we are made parties to it, and *must be* parties to it, whether we like it or not."

The manner in which Dickens makes this great Chancery suit the centre of the story; the manner in which he makes it affect nearly all the characters, from Jo the crossing sweeper to Lady Honoria Dedlock; the manner in which all the abuses of the procedure of the court are naturally introduced into the story—unite to make *Bleak House* the greatest triumph of his art.

Let us now consider a little more in detail some of the abuses of the procedure of the court which are especially illustrated by *Bleak House*. I shall take (1) the Bill; (2) the mode of taking evidence; (3) the Masters and the Six Clerks; (4) the procedure in court; (5) the attempt to do complete justice and its effects; (6) process.

The filing of the Bill was the first step in the case. It contained the plaintiff's statement of his case. It is not particularly described by Dickens; but it is graphically and accurately described by Lord Bowen.* "A bill was a marvellous document, which stated the plaintiff's case at full length, and

* *Select Essays in Anglo American Legal History*, I, 524.

three times over. There was first the part in which the story was circumstantially set forth. Then came the part which charged its truth against the defendant—or, in other words, which set it forth all over again in an aggrieved tone. Lastly came the interrogatory part, which converted the original allegations into a chain of subtly penned interrogatories addressed to the defendant." In the course of the many years that a suit in equity might last, there occurred deaths, births, and marriages. That meant that new bills must be filed to bring the new parties before the court. As Lord Bowen says,* "Whenever any death occurred, bills of review or supplemental suits became necessary to reconstitute the charmed circle of the litigants which had been broken. . . . It was satirically declared that a suit to which fifty defendants were necessary parties . . . could never hope to end at all, since the yearly average of deaths in England was one in fifty, and a death, as a rule, threw over the plaintiff's bill for at least a year." Dickens has picturesquely described this state of things:†

Innumerable children have been born into the

* *Select Essays in Anglo American Legal History,* I, 526.
† *Bleak House,* chap. ii.

cause; innumerable young people have married into it; innumerable old people have died out of it. Scores of persons have deliriously found themselves made parties in Jarndyce and Jarndyce, without knowing how or why; whole families have inherited legendary hatreds with the suit. The little plaintiff or defendant, who was promised a new rocking-horse when Jarndyce and Jarndyce should be settled, has grown up, possessed himself of a real horse, and trotted away into the other world. Fair wards of court have faded into mothers and grandmothers; a long procession of Chancellors has come in and gone out; the legion of bills in the suit have been transformed into mere bills of mortality; there are not three Jarndyces left upon the earth perhaps, since old Tom Jarndyce in despair blew his brains out at a coffee-house in Chancery Lane.

I shall summarize what I have said at greater length in my history,* as to the mode of taking evidence.

The first step was to prepare the interrogatories. These were prepared by the plaintiff's and defendant's counsel. As counsel could not tell what the answers of the witnesses would be, they were necessarily lengthy and minute; and for the same reason the number of the witnesses was often

* Holdsworth, *Hist. Engl. Law,* IX, 354-358.

multiplied unnecessarily. Then the commissioners must be appointed. These commissioners and their clerks then repaired to an inn at the place where the examination was to take place. There they lived at the expense of the parties during the whole time that the examination took place. Each commissioner was paid at the rate of two guineas a day, and each clerk at the rate of fifteen shillings, in addition to his expenses at the inn. There was also two guineas a day to each of the solicitors, and the expenses of the witnesses. At the examination the witnesses were examined "without the presence of the solicitor, or any one representing the parties, or any one acquainted with the circumstances of the case, to see that all the information wanted was drawn forth." The interrogatories were always expressed in very technical language, so that often the witnesses did not understand their meaning. The evidence given was put into the third person, and the phrasing was generally that of the commissioners; so that there was every chance that, in the course of this transposition, its effect would be materially altered. At the close of the examination of each witness, his depositions were engrossed and signed by him. When all the witnesses had been examined—

a process which often took many months—the depositions were sealed up and sent to the court; and thus, as Bentham pointed out, the person who took the evidence had nothing to do with the work of applying it to its proper use. It is obvious that, under these circumstances, cross-examination was useless if not dangerous.

After the depositions were all returned to the court an order of the court was got for their publication. This might be delayed by a motion to enlarge the time allowed for publication, if it appeared that further evidence was needed. Further delays might be caused by a motion, before publication, to suppress depositions. Generally no further evidence could be taken after publication, as it was supposed that if this was allowed it would lead to subornation of perjury; but, even after publication, leave might be given on special motion to take a fresh examination as to the credit of a particular witness.

The slowness of this system is obvious. It is equally obvious that it was both costly and inefficient. Unnecessary numbers of witnesses were examined at great expense; and their testimony was often the reverse of satisfactory, because they did not understand the questions put to them. Two concrete illustrations will suffice to illustrate these two defects. Mr. Lowe, in his evidence to the Chancery Commission, cited a case in which, though there was absolutely no dispute, the cost of examining wholly unnecessary witnesses to prove a will was £100. Mr. Vizard, another witness, said, "I had received a written statement from a witness living in the county of Devon, as to information he could give; I had other means of ascertaining that the information he sent to me was correct; I, in consequence, brought him to town to be examined at a very considerable expense; he went before the examiner and was examined; and when the depositions came to be published, I found the information which he had given directly opposite to that I had expected; upon which I sent him a copy of his letter to me, and a copy of the evidence he had given, and asked him to account for the difference; the explanation I received was that he had wholly mistaken the question as it was put to him."

This mode of taking evidence was so futile that it was necessary to invent some method of getting the facts before the court. Two methods had been invented—one by the court, and the other by the parties, which really extracted evidence, but which added to the length and expense of a suit in equity.

The method invented by the court was the device of settling a disputed question of fact by sending an issue to be tried by a court of common law. At the end of the eighteenth century, the practice was constantly resorted to by the chancellor. "So sensible," wrote Blackstone,* "is the court of the deficiency of trial by written depositions, that it will not bind the parties thereby, but usually directs the matter to be tried by a jury; especially such important facts as the validity of a will, or whether A is heir-at-law to B. . . . But as no jury can be summoned to attend this court, the fact is usually directed to be tried at the bar of the court of king's bench or at the assizes, upon a *feigned issue*. For, (in order to bring it there, and have the point in dispute, and that only, put in issue) an action is feigned to be brought, wherein the pretended plaintiff declares that he laid a wager of £5 with the defendant, that A was the heir-at-law to B; and then avers that he is so; and brings his action for the £5. The defendant allows the wager, but avers that A is not the heir to B; and thereupon that issue is joined, which is

* *Comm.*, III, 452.

directed out of Chancery to be tried; and thus the verdict of the jurors at law determines the fact in the court of equity."

The method invented by the parties was explained by Mr. Lowe in his evidence to the Chancery Commission of 1826. He was asked, "Do you avoid going before the examiner whenever you can?" He replied, "Certainly; and that is one of the reasons that I amend my bills. I get from the defendant by answers all the facts."* And, in answer to another question he said,† "it frequently happens that it is absolutely necessary to scrape the defendant's conscience by continuing to amend the bill: I have amended a bill against one of the first merchants in the city of London three times, in one of the plainest cases that ever was; for that I was very much abused; at last he could not evade the questions put to him, and paid my client the thousand pounds in dispute." It would appear from Bentham that this was generally considered to be a very much more efficient mode of extracting evidence than the regular mode of examining witnesses before an examiner or commissioners.‡

* *Parlt. Papers* (1826), vol. XV, App. A, p. 167.
† *Ibid.*, p. 165. ‡ *Works* (Ed. Bowring), VII, 525.

In the course of a suit it was generally necessary to refer very various matters to the masters of the court. It was in the masters' offices that some of the worst delays took place, and the greatest expense was incurred.*

The procedure before the masters was almost inconceivably dilatory. For every attendance at a master's office a warrant must be taken out, and a fee paid. It was the custom, on leaving the papers to be copied, to take out a warrant for attendance. But, if the papers to be copied were long, the solicitor knew that they could not be ready in time, and so the custom sprang up of never attending till the second, third, or even the fourth warrant. Each attendance was only for an hour; and though, if all the parties were friendly, two or three successive hours might be arranged, this was seldom possible owing to the engagements of the master. If the parties were not friendly the hour would never be exceeded; and the business might be infinitely protracted by failure to attend or to attend punctually. For it would seem that the master's powers to deal with defaulters were very slight. In particular, they had for a long time no

* See *Taff Vale Ry. Co.* v. *Nixon* (1847), 1 H. L. C. at p. 126, *per* Lord Campbell.

power to proceed in the absence of the parties; and, when they got that power, they did not use it; so that if two out of three solicitors attended and the third did not, nothing could be done, though the client was obliged to pay the fees of the two who had attended.*

This procedure took its rise at a time when the master and his clerks were paid by fees for each piece of work done. Every warrant, every copy, every report, carried its fee. This led to the abuse of compelling the suitor to take office copies, which permeated the whole system of Chancery procedure. It is true that this mode of remunerating the masters had ceased in 1833; but the system was still in force when *Bleak House* was written; and the Act of 1833 had done little to remedy the abuse. All that it had effected was to transfer the fees to a fee fund, so that the old procedure and the old fees still remained.† It was for this reason that it was to the interest of the master to lengthen his report, and to adhere to a needlessly complicated method of taking accounts. And this, in its turn, led to many opportunities for

* See Holdsworth, *Hist. Engl. Law,* IX, 360-361, and the references there cited.

† *Ibid.*, p. 362.

motions to the court excepting to the master's report. It was proved in 1826 that the expense incurred in the master's offices amounted to nearly half the expenses of the whole suit.*

The Six Clerks were originally supposed to act as the attorneys of the parties. During the eighteenth century this duty devolved upon their deputies the Sixty Clerks; and, at the end of the eighteenth century the parties employed their own solicitors. But traces of the old system survived in the fees paid by the suitors. Every suitor was obliged to appoint a clerk in court, who was supposed to act as his solicitor in court, to advise his private solicitor, and from whom copies of the pleadings must be obtained. Though the fees paid to these clerks in court amounted to an insignificant sum, compared with the vast sums which were spent in the masters' offices, they all added to the expense; and they obviously tended to increase the delay of a suit. One solicitor told the Chancery Commissioners that he paid them annually about £200 a year out of the money of his clients; and many witnesses agreed that they were wholly useless. That these witnesses were right can be seen from the fact that it was quite a usual

* See Holdsworth, *Hist. Engl. Law,* IX, 365.

occurrence for the same clerk in court to act for adverse parties; and from Mr. Lowe's statement in his evidence to the Chancery Commission, that a "Mr. Shaddick was a good clerk in court even when he was a lunatic." Indeed as he pointed out he had reason to regret the lunatic, "His successor has, since his declared lunacy, got my bills from the office, and has doubled the charges for attendance. It is shameful the way they get money from us and the suitors for ideal attendances."*

Dickens knew something of these facts when he wrote, "From the master, upon whose impaling files reams of dusty warrants in Jarndyce and Jarndyce have grimly writhed into many shapes; down to the copying-clerk in the Six Clerks' Office, who has copied his tens of thousands of Chancery-folio-pages under that eternal heading; no man's nature has been made better by it. In trickery, evasion, procrastination, spoliation, botheration, under false pretences of all sorts, there are influences which can never come to good."†

* See Holdsworth, *Hist. Engl. Law,* IX, 370, and references there cited.

† *Bleak House,* chap. i.

A case came many times before the court; for at all stages motions might be made for many purposes. Maddock, in his book on the Chancery, gives a list of thirteen motions which might be made by a plaintiff after the bill was filed and before answer, and a list of fourteen motions which might be made after demurrer, plea or answer. And any number of counsel could be briefed at the hearing of these motions. Dickens has given us two graphic pictures of a scene in court at the hearing of these motions:

> Thus, in the midst of the mud and at the heart of the fog, sits the Lord High Chancellor in his High Court of Chancery.
>
> "Mr. Tangle," says the Lord High Chancellor, latterly something restless under the eloquence of that learned gentleman.
>
> "Mlud," says Mr. Tangle. Mr. Tangle knows more of Jarndyce and Jarndyce than anybody. He is famous for it—supposed never to have read anything else since he left school.
>
> "Have you nearly concluded your argument?"
>
> "Mlud, no—variety of points—feel it my duty tsubmit—ludship," is the reply that slides out of Mr. Tangle.
>
> "Several members of the bar are still to be heard, I believe?" says the Chancellor, with a slight smile.

Eighteen of Mr. Tangle's learned friends, each armed with a little summary of eighteen hundred sheets, bob up like eighteen hammers in a pianoforte, make eighteen bows, and drop into their eighteen places of obscurity.

"We will proceed with the hearing on Wednesday fortnight," says the Chancellor. For the question at issue is only a question of costs, a mere bud on the forest tree of the parent suit, and really will come to a settlement one of these days.*

The Lord Chancellor threw down a bundle of papers from his desk to the gentlemen below him, and somebody said, "*Jarndyce and Jarndyce.*" Upon this there was a buzz, and a laugh, and a general withdrawal of the bystanders, and a bringing in of great heaps, and piles, and bags and bags full of papers.

I think it came on "for further directions,"—about some bill of costs, to the best of my understanding, which was confused enough. But I counted twenty-three gentlemen in wigs, who said they were "in it"; and none of them appeared to understand it much better than I. They chatted about it with the Lord Chancellor, and contradicted and explained among themselves, and some of them said it was this way, and some of them said it was that way, and some of them jocosely proposed to read huge volumes of affi-

* *Bleak House,* chap. i.

davits, and there was more buzzing and laughing, and everybody concerned was in a state of idle entertainment, and nothing could be made of it by anybody. After an hour or so of this, and a good many speeches being begun and cut short, it was "referred back for the present," as Mr. Kenge said, and the papers were bundled up again, before the clerks had finished bringing them in.*

Finally it should be noticed that all these causes of delay were aggravated, at the period at which the scene of the story is laid, by the fact that the judicial staff of the court was so inadequate that much time elapsed between the time when the case was ready for hearing, and the time when it was actually heard. Since a case came before the court many times at different stages, this waiting time increased enormously the existing delays. In fact the time consumed in merely waiting to be heard amounted almost to a denial of justice. C. P. Cooper writing in 1828 said,† "Two briefs in causes on Further Directions set down before the Vice-Chancellor are at this moment on my table. The real and personal estates in both cases are considerable, and neither the legatees nor residu-

* *Bleak House,* chap. xxiv. † *Chancery,* p. 92.

ary legatees have yet received any part of their bequests. In one suit the bill was filed rather more, and in the other rather less than twenty years since, and, during more than half that time, the causes have, in different stages, been waiting their turn to be heard."

Of the attempt to do complete justice and its effects I have already said something. The court refused to act at all unless it took charge of the whole matter. In the simplest case, it might be a mere question of the construction of a sentence in a will, it administered the whole estate, and compelled the parties (however friendly they might be) to go through all the forms of a hostile suit. Dickens has dealt with this aspect of the Chancery procedure in the tale which Gridley, the man from Shropshire, tells to John Jarndyce:*

"Mr. Jarndyce," he said, "consider my case. As true as there is a Heaven above us, this is my case. I am one of two brothers. My father (a farmer) made a will, and left his farm and stock, and so forth, to my mother, for her life. After my mother's death, all was to come to me, except a legacy of three hundred pounds that I was then to pay my brother. My mother

* *Bleak House,* chap. xv.

died. My brother, some time afterwards, claimed his legacy. I, and some of my relations, said that he had had a part of it already, in board and lodging, and some other things. Now mind! That was the question, and nothing else. No one disputed the will; no one disputed anything but whether part of that three hundred pounds had been already paid or not. To settle that question, my brother filing a bill, I was obliged to go into this accursed Chancery; I was forced there, because the law forced me, and would let me go nowhere else. Seventeen people were made defendants to that simple suit! It first came on, after two years. It was then stopped for another two years, while the Master (may his head rot off!) inquired whether I was my father's son—about which there was no dispute at all with any mortal creature. He then found out that there were not defendants enough—remember, there were only seventeen as yet!—but that we must have another who had been left out; and must begin all over again. The costs at that time—before the thing was begun!—were three times the legacy. My brother would have given up the legacy, and joyful, to escape more costs. My whole estate, left to me in that will of my father's, has gone in costs. The suit, still undecided, has fallen into rack, and ruin, and despair, with everything else—and here I stand, this day!"

"My whole estate, left to me in that will of my father's, has gone in costs." That was the inevitable end of many Chancery suits. Mr. Bickersteth, in his evidence before the Chancery Commission said, "Cases have occurred within my own knowledge in which the whole property sought to be administered in Chancery has proved insufficient to pay the costs of the suit; and in which the last question discussed in the cause has been how the deficient fund was to be apportioned among the different solicitors in part payment of their respective bills."* This was what happened in *Jarndyce* v. *Jarndyce*. It is no doubt true that the discovery of a missing will could not have put a summary end to the case; for, as Sir F. Pollock has said, "Every tyro in equity practice knows that the only immediate effect must have been to add one or more parties to the suit."† But I do not think that Dickens suggests this. It is clear that the suit had ended, before the effect of the missing will was considered, because the whole estate had been absorbed in costs; and this does represent what must have been a not uncommon

* *Parlt. Papers* (1826), vol. XV, App. A, p. 217, cited Holdsworth, *Hist. Engl. Law,* IX, 374.

† *Wigmore Celebration Legal Essays,* p. 17.

occurrence. Here is Dickens's account of the matter:

"Is this Will considered a genuine document, sir?" said Allan; "will you tell us that?"

"Most certainly, if I could," said Mr. Kenge; "but we have not gone into that, we have not gone into that."

"We have not gone into that," repeated Mr. Vholes, as if his low inward voice were an echo.

"You are to reflect, Mr. Woodcourt, that this has been a great cause, that this has been a protracted cause, that this has been a complex cause. Jarndyce and Jarndyce has been termed, not inaptly, a Monument of Chancery practice."

"And Patience has sat upon it a long time," said Allan.

"Very well indeed, sir," returned Mr. Kenge, with a certain condescending laugh he had. "Very well! You are further to reflect, Mr. Woodcourt," becoming dignified almost to severity, "that on the numerous difficulties, contingencies, masterly fictions, and forms of procedure in this great cause, there has been expended study, ability, eloquence, knowledge, intellect, Mr. Woodcourt, high intellect. For many years, the—a—I would say the flower of the Bar, and the—a—I would presume to add, the matured autumnal fruits of the Woolsack—have been lavished upon Jarndyce and

Jarndyce. If the public have the benefit, and if the country have the adornment, of this great Grasp, it must be paid for in money or money's worth, sir."

"Mr. Kenge," said Allan, appearing enlightened all in a moment. "Excuse me, our time presses. Do I understand that the whole estate is found to have been absorbed in costs?"

"Hem! I believe so," returned Mr. Kenge. "Mr. Vholes, what do *you* say?"

"I believe so," said Mr. Vholes.

"And that thus the suit lapses and melts away?"

"Probably," returned Mr. Kenge. "Mr. Vholes?"

"Probably," said Mr. Vholes.*

Enormous were the delays of the process used to get an unwilling defendant before the court, to enforce an answer, and to enforce obedience to a decree.† But the worst consequence of the last named process was this: if the defendant had no estate, or not sufficient estate, he could be imprisoned, and, as Mr. Bickersteth pointed out to the Chancery Commission, he might remain in gaol for the rest of his life.‡ This was what most stirred Dickens's wrath—as witness his account

* *Bleak House,* chap. lxv.

† Holdsworth, *Hist. Engl. Law,* IX, 348-353.

‡ *Parlt. Papers* (1826), vol. XV, App. A, p. 150.

of the sad case of the cobbler in the Fleet prison, who had been the executor of a will, contested first in the ecclesiastical courts, and then in the court of Chancery:*

"Well," said the cobbler, "he left five thousand pounds behind him."

"And wery gen-teel in him so to do," said Sam.

"One of which," continued the cobbler, "he left to me, 'cause I'd married his relation, you see."

"Wery good," murmured Sam.

"And being surrounded by a great number of nieces and nevys, as was always a quarrelling and fighting among themselves for the property, he makes me his executor, and leaves the rest to me: in trust, to divide it among 'em as the will provided."

"Wot do you mean by leavin' it on trust?" inquired Sam, waking up a little. "If it ain't ready money, where's the use on it?"

"It's a law term, that's all," said the cobbler.

"I don't think that," said Sam, shaking his head. "There's wery little trust at that shop. Hows'ever, go on."

"Well," said the cobbler: "when I was going to take out a probate of the will, the nieces and nevys, who was desperately disappointed at not getting all the money, enters a caveat against it."

* *Pickwick,* chap. xliv.

"What's that?" inquired Sam.

"A legal instrument, which is as much as to say, it's no go," replied the cobbler.

"I see," said Sam, "a sort of brother-in-law o' the have-his-carcase. Well."

"But," continued the cobbler, "finding that they couldn't agree among themselves, and consequently couldn't get up a case against the will, they withdrew the caveat, and I paid all the legacies. I'd hardly done it, when one nevy brings an action to set the will aside. The case comes on, some months afterwards, afore a deaf old gentleman, in a back room somewhere down by Paul's Churchyard; and arter four counsels had taken a day a-piece to bother him regularly, he takes a week or two to consider, and read the evidence in six vollums, and then gives his judgment that how the testator was not quite right in his head, and I must pay all the money back again, and all the costs. I appealed; the case come on before three or four very sleepy gentlemen, who had heard it all before in the other court, where they're lawyers without work; the only difference being, that, there, they're called doctors, and in the other place delegates, if you understand that,* and they very dutifully confirmed the decision of the old gentleman below. After that, we went into

* This description of the composition of the High Court of Delegates is perfectly accurate, Holdsworth, *Hist. Engl. Law* (3d ed.), I, 605.

Chancery, where we are still, and where I shall always be. My lawyers have had all my thousand pound long ago; and what between the estate, as they call it, and the costs, I'm here for ten thousand, and shall stop here, till I die, mending shoes. Some gentlemen have talked of bringing it afore parliament, and I dare say would have done it, only they hadn't time to come to me, and I hadn't power to go to them, and they got tired of my long letters, and dropped the business. And this is God's truth, without one word of suppression or exaggeration, as fifty people, both in this place and out of it, very well know."

It was the contrast between the smug complacency and respectability of the court, and the ruin which it brought upon all persons and things which it got within its grasp, which inspired Dickens's pen.

To see everything going on so smoothly, and to think of the roughness of the suitors' lives and deaths; to see all that full dress and ceremony, and to think of the waste, and want, and beggared misery it represented; to consider that, while the sickness of hope deferred was raging in so many hearts, this polite show went calmly on from day to day, and year to year, in such good order and composure; to behold the Lord Chancellor, and the whole array of practitioners under him, looking at one another and at the spectators, as if nobody had ever heard that all over England the name in which they were assembled was a bitter jest: was held in universal horror, contempt, and indignation: was known for something so flagrant and bad, that little short of a miracle could bring any good out of it to any one.*

It was this lesson which Dickens drove into the minds of his readers by his descriptions of the tragic death of Tom Jarndyce, of the life of poor half-crazed Miss Flite, of the effect produced on the character of Richard Carstone by his growing interest in the fatal suit.

As I have already pointed out, some reforms had been made when *Bleak House* was written. But, as the Chancery Commission of 1850 proved, much remained to be done. In fact, at the very time when *Bleak House* began to appear (March, 1852), things were going badly in the Court of Chancery. Mr. Atlay says:† "The existence in its full integrity of the historical office of Lord Chancellor was never in greater peril. The prolonged illness of Lord Cottenham and the habits of procrastination which he developed during his later days had once more piled up the arrears in Chan-

* *Bleak House,* chap. xxiv.

† *Victorian Chancellors,* I, 450.

cery. The issuing of new Orders, the increase in the judicial staff, even the abolition of the Six Clerks' Office, had been powerless to cope with the evil. Never had the public mind been more inflamed; a competent observer declared that the most popular measure which could be introduced into the House of Commons would be one for the abolition *sans phrase* of the Court of Chancery."

But relief was at hand. The result of the Chancery Commission of 1850 was the Chancery Procedure Acts of 1852.* They reformed both the pleading of the court, and its system of procedure. The form of the Bill was changed. It was to consist of a concise narrative of material facts divided into numbered paragraphs, and it was not to contain interrogatories. The masters, and the cumbrous machinery of the masters' offices, were abolished. Their duties were handed over to the judges sitting in Chambers, and to their chief clerks. Certain powers, formerly belonging only to the common law courts, were given to the Court of Chancery, and *vice versa,* so that the Court of Chancery could no longer hang up a suit by sending a case for the consideration of the common law courts. The changes made by these acts in equity

* 15 & 16 Victoria, c.c. 80, 86.

procedure, and by the contemporary Common Law Procedure Acts in common law procedure, paved the way to the fusion of jurisdiction effected by the Judicature Act in 1875, and to the formation of the modern code of procedure contained in the rules of the Supreme Court. Of these reforms I shall have something more to say after I have examined, in the next lecture, the procedure of the common law.

IV.

Pickwick *and the Procedure of the Common Law.*

IN 1827 the procedure of the common law courts was perhaps the most artificial and the most encumbered with fictions that any legal system has ever possessed. Its main rules were mediæval. But these rules, having become unsuited to a more complex society, had been overlaid with a number of conventional practices and legal fictions. The result was that the real working rules of practice had come to depend upon the conventions of the law courts, just as truly as the real working rules of constitutional law had come to depend on the conventions of the constitution.

The mediæval scheme of common law procedure was shortly as follows: The whole scheme centered round the original writs. The suitor must select the writ appropriate to his cause of action. He must then get the defendant before the court by means of the process prescribed for the particular writ which he had selected. When he had got him before the court he must "declare," or "count" against him. The defendant must then plead; and the plaintiff must reply. By means of this oral altercation at the bar, which was recorded as the case proceeded, an issue of law or of fact was reached. The issue of law was decided by the court. The issue of fact was decided in almost all cases by a verdict of a jury, who, being chosen from the neighborhood of the occurrence, were supposed to know the facts, and were, for that reason, as much witnesses to as judges of the facts. On the verdict of the jury the court gave the judgment which, having regard to the record and the law applicable thereto, appeared to be just.

It was a system of procedure suited only to a system of law which was still in an early stage of development. Before the close of the mediæval period, it was already becoming inadequate to the new needs of a more complex society, and a more developed system of law. But the Legislature did very little to bring it up to date. Hence it was, that, at the close of the mediæval period, we can see the beginnings of changes in practice which will, without directly changing the old system, gradually modify it; and, in the end, under cover of numerous fictions and tortuous devices, completely undermine it.

Thus, in the course of the sixteenth and seventeenth centuries, many of the older writs dropped out of use; and trespass and its offshoots usurped the place occupied by the older real and personal actions. Partly owing to this cause, and partly by the direct action of the Legislature, the mesne process upon these writs was shortened and assimilated. For the oral altercation in court between the parties, in which the issue was settled, the system of written pleadings was substituted. The practice of summoning witnesses to testify to the court, and the consequent growth of a law of evidence, revolutionized the conduct of a trial, and changed the whole position of the jury. But, as these changes took place without any direct change in the older system, they could only be fitted on to it by means of the conventional practices or fictions to which I have referred.

In Dickens's account of the progress of the action which Mrs. Bardell brought against Pickwick, we are introduced to three of the leading characteristics of common law procedure and practice. In the first place, we are introduced to some of the conventional practices and fictions of the courts. In the second place, we are introduced to the effects of the rule of the law of evidence, which prevented the parties to an action, or anyone interested in the result of the action, from giving evidence. In the third place, we are introduced to the rules as to the manner in which a judgment could be executed; and, in that connection, to the facility with which a creditor could arrest his debtor. In this lecture I shall deal with these three characteristics of the common law procedure of Dickens's day; and, in conclusion, I shall draw a comparison between the defects of the equity and the common law procedure.

Five of the conventional practices and fictions are alluded to in *Pickwick*. First, the method of starting the proceedings; secondly, the steps taken to secure the appearance of the defendant; thirdly, the effect of certain of the rules of pleading; fourthly, rules as to judgment and its execution; and, fifthly, certain incidents of the trial.

In theory all actions began by the issue of the appropriate original writ; and, if the wrong writ was chosen, the action was lost. In practice, however, plaintiffs very rarely began their actions by the issue of an original writ. This was due to the fact that the use of an original writ was the most expensive and dilatory way of beginning an action, and exposed a plaintiff to greater risks of failure through some merely formal defect. The result was that various devious ways of beginning an action had been invented. The commissioners appointed to report upon the Courts of Common Law stated in 1829 that it was possible to begin an action in the King's Bench and the Common Pleas in five different ways, and in the Exchequer in six different ways. The commissioners pointed out that this complexity was due mainly to three causes—the desire to avoid the expense and inconvenience of the original writ; the desire of the King's Bench and the Exchequer to encroach on the domain of the Common Pleas; and the privilege, allowed to attorneys and other officers of the courts, of suing and being sued in the courts to which they were officially attached.*

Of all these methods of beginning an action the most common was a *capias ad respondendum,* i.e., a writ directing the sheriff to arrest the defendant. This process was possible in all the most usual personal actions; and, where it was possible, it became the practice, in the course of the eighteenth century, to "resort to it in the first instance, and to suspend the issuing of the original writ, or

* Holdsworth, *Hist. Engl. Law,* IX, 249-250.

even to neglect it altogether, unless its omission should afterwards be objected by the defendant. Thus the usual *practical* mode of commencing a personal action by original writ is to begin by issuing, not an original, but a capias."*

This was the course adopted by Dodson and Fogg:

"The writ, sir, which commences the action," continued Dodson, "was issued regularly. Mr. Fogg, where is the *præcipe* book?"

"Here it is," said Fogg, handing over a square book, with a parchment cover.

"Here is the entry," resumed Dodson. " 'Middlesex, Capias *Martha Bardell, widow,* v. *Samuel Pickwick.* Damages, £1500. Dodson and Fogg for the plaintiff, Aug. 28, 1827.' All regular, sir; perfectly."†

It was a very old principle of the common law that there could be no proceedings against an absent defendant. Naturally, from an early date, the law was much concerned with the steps which a plaintiff could take to make a defendant appear, and with the possibility of realizing his claim in the defendant's absence. At the beginning of the eighteenth century the ground was already cumbered by many complex rules, as to different ex-

* *Parlt. Papers* (1829), IX, 77.

† *Pickwick,* chap. xx; see below, p. 127.

pedients, which were applicable to different forms of action. In certain cases, indeed, it had been enacted in 1725 that the plaintiff might, on affidavit that a copy of the process had been personally served, enter an appearance for the defendant.* But, if this procedure was not possible, the plaintiff must choose, according to the nature of his action, or the person who was defendant, or the court in which he brought his action, between distringas, i.e. distraint, capias, i.e. arrest, or attachment and commission of rebellion. The process of capias was by far the most common; and it gave rise to a most complex body of law as to the bail below, i.e. bail which the defendant (if he wished to get released) must give to the sheriff who had made the arrest, for his appearance at the return of the writ; and the bail above, i.e. bail which he must give in court, that he would satisfy judgment. On the acceptance of bail above, the bail below was vacated. But, if the persons accepted by the sheriff as bail below were insolvent, the plaintiff could call on the sheriff to produce the defendant; and if the sheriff then failed to cause sufficient bail above to be taken, he was personally liable to the plaintiff.

* 12 George I, c. 29.

This state of the law led to the existence of a set of men called "sham bail," who would for a consideration be bail for anyone. Mr. Pickwick met these men when he was brought to the judge's chambers at Serjeant's Inn, that he might be removed by writ of *habeas corpus* to the Fleet prison.

The people that attracted his attention most, were three or four men of shabby-genteel appearance, who touched their hats to many of the attorneys who passed, and seemed to have some business there, the nature of which Mr. Pickwick could not divine. They were curious-looking fellows. One, was a slim and rather lame man in rusty black, and a white neckerchief; another was a stout burly person, dressed in the same apparel, with a great reddish-black cloth round his neck; a third, was a little weazen drunken-looking body, with a pimply face. They were loitering about, with their hands behind them, and now and then with an anxious countenance whispered something in the ear of some of the gentlemen with papers, as they hurried by. Mr. Pickwick remembered to have very often observed them lounging under the archway when he had been walking past; and his curiosity was quite excited to know to what branch of the profession these dingy-looking loungers could possibly belong.

He was about to propound the question to Namby,

who kept close behind him, sucking a large gold ring on his little finger, when Perker bustled up, and observing that there was no time to lose, led the way into the Inn. As Mr. Pickwick followed, the lame man stepped up to him, and civilly touching his hat, held out a written card, which Mr. Pickwick, not wishing to hurt the man's feelings by refusing, courteously accepted and deposited in his waistcoat-pocket.

"Now," said Perker, turning round before he entered one of the offices, to see that his companions were close behind him. "In here, my dear sir. Hallo, what do *you* want?"

This last question was addressed to the lame man, who, unobserved by Mr. Pickwick, made one of the party. In reply to it, the lame man touched his hat again, with all imaginable politeness, and motioned towards Mr. Pickwick.

"No, no," said Perker with a smile. "We don't want you, my dear friend, we don't want you."

"I beg your pardon, sir," said the lame man. "The gentleman took my card. I hope you will employ me, sir. The gentleman nodded to me. I'll be judged by the gentleman himself. You nodded to me, sir?"

"Pooh, pooh, nonsense. You didn't nod to anybody, Pickwick? A mistake, a mistake," said Perker.

"The gentleman handed me his card," replied Mr. Pickwick, producing it from his waistcoat-pocket. "I accepted it, as the gentleman seemed to wish it—in fact I had some curiosity to look at it when I should be at leisure. I—"

The little attorney burst into a loud laugh, and returning the card to the lame man, informing him it was all a mistake, whispered to Mr. Pickwick as the man turned away in dudgeon, that he was only a bail.

"A what!" exclaimed Mr. Pickwick.

"A bail!" replied Perker.

"A bail!"

"Yes, my dear sir—half a dozen of 'em here. Bail you to any amount, and only charge half-a-crown. Curious trade, isn't it?" said Perker, regaling himself with a pinch of snuff.

"What! Am I to understand that these men earn a livelihood by waiting about here, to perjure themselves before the judges of the land, at the rate of half-a-crown a crime!" exclaimed Mr. Pickwick, quite aghast at the disclosure.

"Why, I don't exactly know about perjury, my dear sir," replied the little gentleman. "Harsh word, my dear sir, very harsh word indeed. It's a legal fiction, my dear sir, nothing more."*

As I have said, Dickens was not a lawyer. He does not therefore attempt to enter upon the intricacies of the rules of pleading. But certain of these

* *Pickwick,* chap. xl.

rules are needed to understand the course of the action in *Bardell* v. *Pickwick.*

The writ, or rather the capias, in that action was issued August 28, 1827, and the trial took place February 14, 1828.* The reason why this delay took place was as follows:—In the Middle Ages the pleadings in an action were settled by an oral altercation in court. This method had been superseded by the practice of exchanging written pleadings. But it is clear that, when the pleadings were settled by an oral altercation in court, they could only be conducted when the court was sitting. That is, they could only be conducted in term time. It is true that the practice had sprung up of filing and delivering pleadings in the vacation as well as in term. But the commissioners who reported on the Courts of Common Law pointed out in 1830 that considerable traces of the mediæval rules remained. All writs had to be made returnable in term time. All pleadings had to be entitled as of some term; and though a plaintiff could declare in vacation, he could not compel the defendant to plead till the next term.† This is the explanation of the delay in hearing the action.

* See *The Times,* Feb. 28, 1928, where it is shown that the dates 1830 and 1831, usually printed in the book, are printer's errors.

† Holdsworth, *Hist. Engl. Law,* IX, 256.

The same causes which led to delays in pleading led to delays in the execution of a judgment. All entries of judgments, though the case was heard, as Pickwick's was, in vacation, must be entered as of some term.* It followed that though Mrs. Bardell got her judgment in vacation she had to wait till the following term to issue execution.

> "No, Perker," said Mr. Pickwick, with great seriousness of manner, "my friends here, have endeavoured to dissuade me from this determination, but without avail. I shall employ myself as usual, until the opposite party have the power of issuing a legal process of execution against me; and if they are vile enough to avail themselves of it, and to arrest my person, I shall yield myself up with perfect cheerfulness and content of heart. When can they do this?"
>
> "They can issue execution, my dear sir, for the amount of the damages and taxed costs, next term," replied Perker, "just two months hence, my dear sir."†

One of the first incidents of the trial was the calling over of the jury, and, on it being discovered that only ten were present, the necessity arose for counsel to "pray," and for the judge to

* Holdsworth, *Hist. Engl. Law,* IX, 257.

† *Pickwick,* chap. xxxv.

"award a tales"—that is to ask the court to order that so many of the bystanders (*tales de circumstantibus*) be impressed, as was necessary to make up the number to twelve. On the order being made the necessary number was impressed. In Coke's day, provided that one of the jury summoned had appeared, the other eleven could be tales-men.* Pickwick's case was tried by a special jury. As Mr. Theobald Mathew has pointed out,† an Act of 1826 (6 George IV, c. 50, §3) had provided that if sufficient special jurymen were not present, the talesmen were to be taken from the common jury. This was what happened when Serjeant Buzfuz prayed a tales:

> This being done, a gentleman in black, who sat below the judge, proceeded to call over the names of the jury; and after a great deal of bawling, it was discovered that only ten special jurymen were present. Upon this, Mr. Serjeant Buzfuz prayed a *tales;* the gentleman in black then proceeded to press into the special jury, two of the common jurymen; and a green-grocer and a chemist were caught directly.
>
> "Answer to your names, gentlemen, that you may

* See Holdsworth, *Hist. Engl. Law* (3d ed.), I, 332, n. 8.

† *Law Quarterly Review,* XXXIV, 323.

be sworn," said the gentleman in black. "Richard Upwitch."

"Here," said the green-grocer.

"Thomas Groffin."

"Here," said the chemist.*

Mr. Mathew has pointed out that Dickens got the idea of this episode from a then recent *cause célèbre:*

On February 11, 1837, there was a non-attendance of the special jurors summoned to deal with the action of *De Roos* v. *Cumming,* in which the noble plaintiff claimed damages for the defamatory statement of the defendant that he had cheated habitually and successfully at cards. As in *Bardell* v. *Pickwick,* the proceedings began with the praying of a *tales,* the Serjeant Buzfuz of the occasion being Mr. Attorney-General Campbell. Less fortunate than Mrs. Bardell, Lord De Roos did not secure the verdict of the mixed jury. He retired to the continent, and was heard of no more. A suggested epitaph—'Here lies Lord De Roos awaiting the Last Trump'—was favourably received by the world of fashion and *ton.*†

On this occasion the chemist objected in vain to serve on the jury on the following ground:

* *Pickwick,* chap. xxxiv.

† *Law Quarterly Review,* XXXIV, 323.

"I've left nobody but an errand boy in my shop. He is a very nice boy, my Lord, but he is not acquainted with drugs; and I know that the prevailing impression on his mind is, that Epsom salts means oxalic acid; and syrup of senna, laudanum."

This is probably an echo of *Tessymond's Case** heard at the Lancaster summer assizes of 1828. In that case a chemist's apprentice was found guilty of manslaughter and fined £5, for negligently causing the death of an infant by selling a bottle of laudanum labelled paregoric, and saying that ten drops were a proper dose.

Another incident of the trial is Dickens's account of the "opening of the case" by Mr. Skimpin. This meant that the counsel merely stated the effect of the pleadings—a mode of conveying information which, as Dickens said, told the jury nothing of the essential facts of the case. "The ushers again called silence, and Mr. Skimpin proceeded to open the case; and the case appeared to have very little inside it when he had opened it, for he kept such particulars as he knew, completely to himself, and sat down after a lapse of three minutes, leaving the jury in precisely the

* 1 Lewin, *Crown Cases,* 169.

same advanced stage of wisdom as they were in before."*

I pass now to the important rule of the law of evidence which is illustrated by the case of *Bardell* v. *Pickwick*.

Readers of the case of *Bardell* v. *Pickwick* have often asked, Why did not the two parties to the action go into the box and tell their respective tales? The answer is that at that date this was legally impossible. The law excluded the evidence of all interested in the result of the action, and *a fortiori* the parties to an action.

This exclusive rule was a rule both of the civil and canon law and of the common law. In the civil and canon law it was based on the fear that, to allow interested persons to testify, would be a direct incitement to perjury. In the common law the rule excluding the evidence of the parties has ancient roots, as Dean Wigmore has shown.† But in the course of the sixteenth century, the rule was justified by the common lawyers on the grounds adopted by the civil and canon lawyers.

* *Pickwick,* chap. xxxiv.

† *System of Evidence* (1st ed.), I, 688-698, §575; cp. Holdsworth, *Hist. Engl. Law,* IX, 193-196.

In *Slade's Case** Coke said, "Experience proves that men's consciences grow so large that the respect of their private advantage rather induces men . . . to perjury." But, if this reasoning is accepted, it will lead to the conclusion arrived at by the civil and canon law, that not only the parties, but also any persons interested in the result of the litigation should be excluded. This reasoning was accepted by Coke, and stated by him as a settled rule of law.† On this matter, as on many other matters, Coke's statement fixed the law. In the eighteenth and nineteenth centuries both the rule and its explanation were well settled. "It is founded," said Starkie in 1824,‡ "on the known infirmities of human nature, which is too weak to be generally restrained by religion or moral obligations, when tempted and solicited in a contrary direction by temporal interests. There are, no doubt, many whom no interests could seduce from a sense of duty, and their exclusion by the operation of this rule may in particular cases shut out the truth. But the law must prescribe general rules; and experience proves that more

* (1602) 4 Co. Rep. at f. 95a. † Co. Litt., 6b.
‡ *Evidence*, p. 83.

mischief would result from the general reception of interested witnesses than is occasioned by their general exclusion."

But the rule was really based on fallacious reasoning, and it led to absurdities in practice. It rested on fallacious reasoning because, as Bentham pointed out,* interest in the result of the litigation is an objection, not to the competence of the witness, but to the weight of his evidence. It led, as Lord Bowen has pointed out,† to absurdities in practice. "The merchant whose name was forged to a bill of exchange had to sit by, silent and unheard, while his acquaintances were called to offer conjectures and beliefs as to the authenticity of the disputed signature from what they knew of his other writings. If a farmer in his gig ran over a foot passenger in the road, the two persons whom the law singled out to prohibit from becoming witnesses were the farmer and the foot-passenger." It was due to the efforts of Denman and Brougham that these objections to the rule were brought to the notice of the public, and that this disqualification of parties to the action and

* *Rationale of Judicial Evidence*, bk. ix, pt. iii, c. iii.

† *Select Essays in Anglo American Legal History*, I, 521.

parties interested was got rid of in the course of the nineteenth century.*

What would have been the result of the case of *Bardell* v. *Pickwick* if the parties could have given evidence? Sir Frank Lockwood contended, in a lecture which he gave on *The Law and Lawyers of Pickwick,* that Pickwick would have taken no benefit—but rather the reverse.† But his views are founded on the erroneous premise that counsel for Mrs. Bardell knew as much of the past history of Pickwick as the readers of the *Pickwick Papers.* This is obviously not true, as is shown by the fact that the unfortunate disclosure made by Winkle of the episode of the mistaken bedroom at Ipswich, came as a complete surprise to Serjeant Buzfuz. And I cannot doubt, first, that a rigid cross-examination of Mrs. Bardell, as to the manner in which she had been persuaded to start proceedings, might have had considerable effect on the jury; and, secondly, that Pickwick's explanation of the circumstances under which Mrs. Bardell was found fainting in his arms, might have convinced them of the truth of his story.

* 6 & 7 Victoria, c. 85—persons interested; 14 & 15 Victoria, c. 99, §2—parties in civil cases; 61 & 62 Victoria, c. 36—parties in criminal cases.

† At p. 82.

I pass now to my third point—the execution of the judgment, and the law as to imprisonment for debt.

When Dickens wrote, the law on these two closely allied topics was in a very curious condition. It was extraordinarily easy for a creditor to arrest his debtor, either as part of mesne process to compel appearance, or in satisfaction of a judgment which he had got against him. Pickwick was taken in execution on the judgment against him; and Mrs. Bardell was taken on a *cognovit actionem*—that is on a recognition by her that the plaintiff had a good cause of action, which recognition had the same operation as a judgment.* Sam Weller got his father to arrest him on mesne process for debt in order that he might attend upon his master in the Fleet prison. That Dickens's picture was not overdrawn is, I think, proved by Lord Bowen's statement. He says:† It was not till after the beginning of the reign [of Queen Victoria] that arrest upon mesne process was abolished, and imprisonment in execution of final

* When Mrs. Bardell signed this document she obviously was wholly ignorant of its effect; a remedy was provided for this abuse in 1838 by 1 & 2 Victoria, c. 110, §9.

† *Select Essays in Anglo American Legal History*, I, 544.

judgments continued to be law till a far more recent date. From October 1, 1838, to December 1, 1839 (a period of fourteen months) 3,905 persons were arrested for debt in London and the provinces, and of these 361 remained permanently in gaol for default of payment or satisfaction. Out of the 3,905 debtors so arrested, dividends were obtained in 199 cases only. The debtor who was left in durance vile shared a common prison with the murderer and the thief, and the spectacle of misfortune linked in this manner to the side of crime was as demoralising as it was cruel." It is quite clear that the institution of the Insolvent Court, to which I alluded in my first lecture,* which could release debtors on terms, was an absolute necessity.

Moreover, as might be expected, this state of the law led to all manner of fraud and chicanery. Listen to the evidence which Mr. Anderton, attorney, and secretary to the Metropolitan Law Society, gave to the commissioners on the Courts of Common Law in 1831. "Almost every man's liberty is liable to be invaded, be his means what they may; clergymen, gentlemen, merchants, and tradesmen are all alike subject to be torn from

* Above, pp. 23-25.

their families, at almost any moment, and arrested for debts they do not owe." Thus, "A respectable merchant . . . was in April, 1826, arrested upon a writ issued by the plaintiff in person for the sum of £60,000, not one sixpence of which he owed; but rather than find bail for so large an amount, and the plaintiff being a man of straw, he submitted to the payment of £100 for his discharge. This having answered so well, he was in the following month again arrested, for £60,000 more, upon which he was discharged by a judge's order upon filing common bail, and no further proceedings were taken in either of the actions. It is true he might have prosecuted the plaintiff for a vexatious arrest, but his doing so would only have increased the expense."*

And what places the prisons were to whom these unfortunate persons were sent!

The Fleet prison compared favorably with other prisons in London and the provincial towns.† For a prisoner, like Pickwick, with money, it could be made at least bearable. And Sugden (the future Lord St. Leonards), in a speech to the House of

* *Parlt. Papers* (1831), vol. X, App. E, p. 220.

† See Bowen, *Select Essays in Anglo American Legal History,* I, 544-545.

Commons on February 11, 1830,* produced some curious cases of prisoners committed for contempt of the Court of Chancery, who occupied lucrative positions in the prison, and preferred to remain there. "The cook had been confined in contempt for six years, although he need not have remained there for six days had he chosen to give up his flourishing office. The hotel keeper had been ten years in prison, without the slightest necessity for stopping there, and his place was worth, he was informed, from £200 to £300 a year. The individual who occupied the tap—a situation worth from £150 to £200 a year—had been committed for contempt, and had already remained there for six years. Another person was a solicitor; he had been in the Fleet three years, and need not have been there as many days; but he was now domiciled and practised his profession with much success." But for the poor prisoners, like Jingle, life was a hell—"they lounged, and loitered, and slunk about, with as little spirit or purpose as the beasts in a menagerie." And everywhere "there were the same squalor, the same turmoil and noise . . . in every corner; in the best and the worst alike. The

* Hansard, 2d Series, XXI, 371, cited by Atlay, *Victorian Chancellors,* II, 15.

whole place seemed restless and troubled; and the people were crowding and flitting to and fro, like the shadows in an uneasy dream."*

There are two points in connection with this subject which I must say a word about. First, a general question, How did English law get itself into this curious condition? Secondly, a more particular question, Why did Dodson and Fogg elect to arrest Pickwick, who was a man of means, instead of levying execution on his property?

The answer to the first question is as follows:† It would seem that originally the common law only admitted of execution against the property of a debtor. By the writ of *fieri facias* the amount could be levied from the goods and chattels of the debtor. By the writ of *levari facias* it could be levied from the goods and profits of the land. By the writ of *elegit* the creditor could take and occupy half the land till he had levied the amount due from it. But the common law soon found that it could not do without some form of personal execution. And, in fact, this form of execution was gradually and indirectly introduced, by means of changes in the process of the courts,

* *Pickwick,* chap. xlv.

† See Holdsworth, *Hist. Engl. Law,* VIII, 230-232.

and changes in, and developments of, the forms of action. The manner of its introduction was as follows:—From the first a writ of *capias ad respondendum* had been a part of mesne process in actions of trespass *vi et armis*. In the thirteenth century this writ was extended to actions of account; in the fourteenth century to actions of debt, detinue, and replevin; and at the beginning of the sixteenth century to actions on the case. It had been laid down in Edward III's reign that when a writ of *capias ad respondendum* lay to get defendant before the court, a writ of *capias ad satisfaciendum* would lie to obtain execution of the judgment. The result was that in practically every case a creditor could take his debtor's body in execution. Constraint of the debtor's person thus became in England a more general method of execution than in any other country in Europe. Largely because it was introduced in this indirect way, a mode of execution which required, and in most countries received, careful attention and regulation from the Legislature, was almost entirely unregulated. This was the cause for the state of things which Dickens has portrayed with a vividness which is only equalled by its truth.

If a creditor elected to arrest his debtor, no

other mode of execution was open to him. Why then did Dodson and Fogg elect to arrest Pickwick who was a man of means? I think that the answer to this question is to be found in the limitations of the three common law writs for taking the property of a debtor in execution—limitations which help to explain the view, then held by many, that these extensive powers to arrest for debt were necessary for the security of creditors. Pickwick had no land, and no tangible chattels of any value. He was a peripatetic person who lived in lodgings and hotels. His means, it would seem, consisted in the income he drew from investments. Now these were choses in action which, because they could not be physically seized, could not be taken under a writ of *fieri facias*. In 1831-1832 the Common Law Procedure Commissioners said,* "The creditor may have execution against all the movable goods of the debtor, but he cannot have execution against copyhold lands, or more than half of the profits of the freehold of the defendant, or against stock in the public funds, or bonds, bills of exchange, or other securities, or any

* *Parlt. Papers* (1831-1832), vol. XXV, pt. i, p. 38. In accordance with the recommendation of the Commissioners the law was altered in 1838, 1 & 2 Victoria, c. 110, §§11 and 12.

debts due to the debtor. . . . The only means which the law at present provides for procuring satisfaction to the creditor, where the debtor's property is of the description before mentioned, is by permitting the arrest and imprisonment of the debtor, until the latter, as the condition of obtaining his liberty, cedes the property for the benefit of the judgment creditor." It followed, therefore, that Dodson and Fogg had really no choice. The only means of making Pickwick pay was to arrest him. It was a master stroke, when they found that this step was not producing the money, to put further pressure on him by arresting Mrs. Bardell, and by sending her to the same prison. Perker's admiration of the cleverness of this step was well deserved; and it is no wonder that, at the end of the story, Dodson and Fogg are left conducting a lucrative business.

In conclusion I should like to compare the defects of the equity and common law procedure which are so strikingly illustrated in these two works of Dickens.*

There are certain points of similarity between

* For further details and the authorities see Holdsworth, *Hist. Engl. Law,* IX, 371-376.

the defects of the equity and common law procedure. Both were old systems which, at the beginning of the nineteenth century, were quite unsuited to modern needs. Both contained many meaningless survivals of old rules. In both the rules of practice were uncodified, and rested on a few orders of the courts, which had in many cases been superseded by the growth of a traditional and conventional practice. Both systems were needlessly expensive. Rules might become obsolete; but if their working carried a fee to an official, the fee remained. In both systems sinecure and salable offices, the work of which was either not done at all, or done by deputy, abounded.

There are also more considerable points of difference between the two systems.

In three points I think that it may be maintained that equity procedure was superior to the common law procedure. First, there was one uniform method of beginning a suit in equity. This contrasted favorably with the multifarious and devious ways by which a common law action could be begun. Secondly, at common law a plaintiff's whole case, whatever might be its intrinsic merits, was staked upon the correctness of the form of the action which his pleader chose to select, and the words which he chose to employ in his pleadings. This was never the case in equity. The Chancellors always tried to decide according to the substantial merits of the case, and a mistake of a word or a form was never irretrievable. Thirdly, the common law modes of questioning the correctness of decisions by writs of error or bills of exceptions were archaic and inconvenient. Equity had from the first adopted the straightforward method of questioning a decision by a rehearing of the case.

But in other respects the advantage rests with the procedure of the common law. Common law process was no doubt permeated with conventions and fictions. But, as I have said in my *History*,* "the conventions and the fictions were in the main directed towards the speedy conduct of the action in accordance with modern needs. On the other hand, the equity rules aimed at the doing of complete justice regardless of any other consideration. No doubt the administrative character of much of the equitable jurisdiction necessitated many more delays than the trial of a common law action. But the delays need not have been so great if the ideal of completeness had not been so high. By aiming at perfection the equity procedure precluded itself

* *Hist. Engl. Law*, IX, 373-374.

from attaining the more possible, if more mundane, ideal of substantial justice. And the ideal aimed at was made the more impossible by the very small control which the Chancellor was able or chose to exercise on the machinery and the officials of his court. As compared with the three courts of common law the judicial strength of the Chancery was ridiculously small. Necessarily control was stricter in the common law courts. Nor was there in the courts of common law the same temptation to delay as there was in the Court of Chancery. In an ordinary common law action there were certain steps to be taken and certain fees to be earned—the sooner those steps were taken and those fees earned the better for all concerned. In many suits in equity large masses of property were in court, and the longer the suit lasted, the more of it went to the officials of the court and the legal advisers of the parties." We have seen that in a contested suit they sometimes absorbed the whole.*

The procedure of the Court of Chancery was less archaic than the procedure of the common law courts. But it was as badly adapted to the needs of the day at the beginning of the nine-

* Above, p. 107.

teenth century as the procedure of these courts. And the Chancellors were not so ready as the common law judges to adapt the procedure of their court to those needs. Their time was too much occupied with their other duties, and their control over their officials was lax. Too many officials had a vested interest in things as they were; and lawyers who understood a system which supplied them with an ample livelihood were likely to rally to its defence. In fact, as I have already said, all the abuses of the court found defenders when it was put upon its trial before the first Chancery Commission. This fact shows that the court and its officials and practitioners had become so close a body, that they had lost touch, in a way in which the common law courts and their officials and practitioners had never lost touch, with the common life and public opinion of the day. Hence, although there was stagnation enough and abuses enough in the common law procedure at the end of the eighteenth century, there was never acquiescence in any such systematic injustice as was perpetrated by the procedure of the Court of Chancery, in its endeavor to accomplish, by means of an utterly inadequate staff and an obsolete machinery, an unattainable ideal of complete justice.

I have now concluded my series of illustrations of the way in which the novels of Charles Dickens throw light on many aspects of the legal history of the first half of the nineteenth century. I hope that it will be agreed that they prove the truth of my opening statement, that they give us information for which we look in vain in the regular authorities; and that they justify my contention that the extent, the variety, and the accuracy of this information entitles us to reckon one of the greatest of our English novelists as a member of the select band of our legal historians.

Addendum

My brother, Mr. C. S. Holdsworth, has pointed out to me, too late for insertion in the text, that Dickens has made a slip in his statement of the law, in Chap. XLVII of *Pickwick*. He makes Perker say:

"I say that nobody but you can rescue her" [Mrs. Bardell] "from this den of wretchedness; and you can only do that by paying the costs of this suit—*both of plaintiff and defendant*—into the hands of these Freeman's Court sharks." But obviously the obligation of the defendant Pickwick was to pay *his* costs to his solicitor Perker. These costs were not payable to the plaintiff's solicitors Dodson and Fogg—the Freeman's Court sharks. The costs payable to Dodson and Fogg were the plaintiff's, Mrs. Bardell's, costs; and it was his refusal to pay these costs which was the cause of his and Mrs. Bardell's arrest. Pickwick could and did rescue Mrs. Bardell by paying her costs—the costs, that is, *of the plaintiff only.*

Index

www.ingramcontent.com/pod-product-compliance
Lightning Source LLC
Chambersburg PA
CBHW021154160426
42812CB00082B/3087/J
9781886363069